# SCHOOL BEGINS AT TWO

# School Begins at Two

## A BOOK FOR TEACHERS
## AND PARENTS

« « « « « « « « « « » » » » » » » » » » »

*From the Manuscripts of*

HARRIET M. JOHNSON

*Edited by* BARBARA BIBER

*for the Bureau of Educational Experiments*

*New York City*

« « « « « « « « « « » » » » » » » » » » »

AGATHON PRESS, INC.

NEW YORK

1970

Original publication, 1936

Reprinted, 1970, by
AGATHON PRESS, INC.
150 Fifth Avenue
New York, N. Y. 10011

New material © 1970 by Agathon Press, Inc.

LC Catalog Card Number: 70-108765

SBN: 87586-022-2

Printed in the United States

## INTRODUCTION TO THE AGATHON EDITION

IT SEEMS fitting that I, who belong to the present generation of early childhood educators, should have been asked to write an introduction to the Agathon edition of *School Begins at Two*. For Harriet Johnson's thinking represents at once the intellectual vigor and humanistic orientation of the traditional and the scientific freshness and experimentalism of the contemporary.

Harriet Johnson exemplified the avant garde of her day. She lived and worked at the frontiers, sharing with her contemporaries in other disciplines a sense of commitment and adventure.

I remember my first encounter with *School Begins at Two*. I was a student teacher engaged in a very personal daily struggle to test out the dimensions around which to shape my beliefs and behaviors as an educator. Harriet Johnson spoke to me with wisdom and simplicity. Her writing had an integrity which has become even more compelling with the passage of time.

What are some of the philosophical and theoretical themes that may be traced in the body of Harriet Johnson's work? Do they have relevance for us now as we struggle to shape educational settings in response to economic and social pressures and in relation to a continuing revolution in technology and communication? I have chosen to enumerate just a few—the reader will of course be struck by others.

1. *The teacher takes responsibility for the climate of the classroom.*

Harriet Johnson takes the view that the teacher is not "a nice lady who likes little children" but a sophisticated theoretician and student of her discipline. The teaching role is presented as a complex one requiring differentiated skills and an intellectual approach. The professional commitment is to structure, nurture and protect the learning environment for the growing child.

2. *Individuality is honored, the child is given time and space and stimulation in which to come to know himself and others.*

Harriet Johnson's goals are broadly based—she sees social significance in the formulation of each individual ego. This approach is indeed child-centered. Harriet Johnson gives this term a particular connotation. She is not sentimental. She deals with the reality of the child's world as he experiences it. Her presentation of very young children has the ring of authenticity.

3. *The school is a special medium designed to promote learning and growth.*

The world of school is dramatic and intense. It is full of encounters and illuminations. The community of the child world is a shared culture with maximum opportunity for individual and group interplay. Life tasks, social graces, manners are intrinsic and supportive.

Harriet Johnson speaks to us from a perspective so removed from our own. One wonders: had she been able to continue her work and study into the present, what aspects of her thinking would she have modified?

As a contemporary educator, I would want to talk to her about the authority role of the teacher. She seems so unconflicted, so unequivocal. I wonder how she would relate to children who are perhaps more impulsive and less verbal than those she describes.

And I would wish very much that she were able today to add another paragraph in relation to cognitive development. Would she make explicit that which is implicit throughout her work? Would she articulate the scope and sequence of cognitive and affective development? Would she further document how these are interrelated?

Harriet Johnson's writings remain a model for educational innovation. She modified theory in relation to practice. She evolved enactment in the light of a continuing critical dialogue with the best minds of her day.

This approach is open-ended and developmental, yet its goals are clearly defined. Harriet Johnson's "instructional objectives," though couched in the vernacular of another generation, have enduring vitality. In this exciting and awesome era of extraterrestrial exploration and behaviorist manipulation it is worthwhile to examine once again the contribution of this educational pioneer.

LORRAINE SMITHBERG
Bank Street College of Education
January, 1970

# TABLE OF CONTENTS

## PART I

|  | PAGE |
|---|---|
| Biographical Account | ix |
| Working Background of Harriet Johnson's Contribution to Education | xii |
| Preschool Curriculum | 5 |
| *Adapting to School Experiences* | 7 |
| The separate functions of home and school | 8 |
| Social codes within the school and beyond it | 13 |
| School routines: eating and sleeping | 15 |
| Maintaining a healthy attitude toward health | 23 |
| The teacher's response to emotional behavior | 24 |
| *The Functions of Play Activity* | 31 |
| Impulses revealed by spontaneous play | 32 |
| Qualities of leadership | 37 |
| Techniques for social participation | 41 |
| Past experience relived through dramatic play | 45 |
| *The Need for Selective Teaching* | 49 |

## PART II

| Foundations for a School Philosophy | 63 |
|---|---|
| *Growth as a Basis for Curriculum* | 63 |
| Each stage of growth has its own needs | 63 |
| Harmonious growth means power to adjust to and exert control over the total environment | 65 |
| Observation of behavior supplies data for studying growth | 69 |

PAGE

*Adaptation as a Goal, in Contrast to Training*                                              78

Acquiring habits of self-help should be a gratifying adventure                               78
What is a realistic balance between manners as a habit and genuine feeling?                   85
Is thumb-sucking a bad habit or a faulty adaptation?                                          95

Working Hypotheses of a Nursery School        100

*Play Activity as a Medium of Growth*          100

Children need to explore and experiment, to create and understand                           101
Play materials serve as tools for expression   105
Dramatic play is the child's way of organizing experience                                   110
Play schemes are a vehicle for constructive social relations                                115

*Extending the Child's Environment*            121

A child can comprehend relations readily when his experience is kept real and simple        121
Trips for children need to be planned toward continuity and relevance of experience         124

*Teacher, Child, and Program*                  130

The teacher's role is distinct from that of the parent                                      131
The teacher's control is a function of her combined skill and understanding                 133
The progressive teacher requires progressive training                                       141

*School: The First Step Beyond the Home*       146

The child's security can be protected in the face of new situations and undertakings        147

PART III

Notes on the Study of Individual Children
in a School Situation                            161
A Study of One Child's Immature Re-
sponse to the Nursery School Environ-
ment                                             161

General physical condition                       164
Visual peculiarities                             165
Level of language responsiveness                 168
Delayed and aborted reactions                    170
Range of social awareness                        175
Absence of dramatic play                         179
Growing language facility                        179
Responsibility for routines                      182
Play activities                                  184

A Developmental Comparison of Two
Children of the Same Age                          190

Postural activities                              192
Language activities                              204
Rhythmic activities                              211
Social activities                                215
Immaturities                                     218

# HARRIET MERRILL JOHNSON

Harriet Merrill Johnson was born in Portland, Maine, on August 28, 1867. In 1871 the family moved to Bangor, Maine, where Harriet attended the public schools and later taught for several years in a private school.

In 1895 Miss Johnson entered the Massachusetts Homeopathic Hospital for a nurses' training course. After graduation she spent two years in private nursing and two years as superintendent of nurses' training at the Homeopathic Hospital in Biddeford, Maine. In 1902 she went to Teachers College, Columbia, for further study in Nursing and Health which work led her to district nursing at Hartley House, New York, under the auspices of the Henry Street Settlement.

In 1905 Miss Johnson became interested in the problems of maladjusted children in public schools. She helped the Public Education Association to organize the Visiting Teachers staff of which she became the head. She left to become a member of the staff of the Psychological Survey, an investigation conducted in various public schools.

In 1917 Miss Johnson acted as adviser to a small nursery school which she, along with five parents, had organized at Greenwich House.

In the same year, 1917, Harriet Johnson, Caroline Pratt and Lucy Sprague Mitchell organized the Bureau of Educational Experiments. During the following seventeen years until her death in 1934, she was a member of the Bureau staff in the following capacities:

1917-1934 Member of the Working Council.

1917-1934 Member of the Research Staff.

1917-1919 General Secretary.

1919-1930 Director of the Bureau Nursery School.

1930-1934 Co-director with Jessie Stanton of the Bureau Nursery School.

1930-1934 Member of teaching faculty of the Cooperative School for Student Teachers.

1930-1934 Member of the Central Staff of the Cooperative School for Student Teachers.

1932-1934 Co-editor of the Cooperating School Pamphlets.

In 1934, after Miss Johnson's death, educators and professional and personal friends established the Harriet Johnson Memorial Fund with Winifred Lenihan as chairman. Miss Emily Child has represented the Memorial Committee in assisting with the preparation of the present manuscript, "School Begins at Two."

*Publications:*

### BOOKS

Children in the Nursery School. The John Day Co., N. Y., 1928.

* School Begins at Two. New Republic, N. Y., 1936.

* Published after Miss Johnson's death.

ARTICLES AND MONOGRAPHS

The Art of Block Building
  Cooperating School Pamphlets, No. 1, The John
  Day Co., 1933.
A Nursery School Health Program
  Practical Home Economics, September, 1931.
Dramatic Play in the Nursery School
  Progressive Education, January, 1931.
Creative Materials for the Preschool Child
  American Childhood, January, 1931.
Play Materials for the Preschool Child
  American Childhood, December, 1930.
Pioneer Babies in the New Education
  American Childhood, February, 1930.
Responsibilities for the Young Child
  Child Study, January, 1928.
The Education of the Nursery School Child
  Childhood Education, November, 1926.
Educational Implications of the Nursery School
  Progressive Education, January-February-March,
  1925.
A Nursery School Experiment
  Published by the Bureau of Educational Experi-
  ments, N. Y. C., 1924.
The Visiting Teacher in New York City
  Published by Public Education Association of the
  City of New York, 1916.

# THE WORKING BACKGROUND
# OF HARRIET JOHNSON'S
# CONTRIBUTION TO EDUCATION

Nowadays, nursery schools are more or less taken for granted as undertakings appropriate even for federal emergency relief, though, of course, they are not universally approved of. But eighteen years ago, in 1917, when Harriet M. Johnson presented her first plan for "An Educational Experiment for Young Children" to the Bureau of Educational Experiments, there was not, so far as we know, a genuine nursery school in America. Miss Macmillan had been using that name in her work with groups of children in England. The main object was relief to working mothers, and the general scheme was an enlargement of the family set-up, with older children helping in the care of younger ones. Harriet Johnson's thinking about nursery schools extended beyond this family need and placed the chief emphasis upon the needs of the children themselves. This was true from the beginning, as indicated in her first plan, to the end, as outlined in a plan she made a few days before her death in February, 1934; and all through the intervening years when she directed the Nursery School of the Bureau of Educational Experiments, now appropriately renamed the Harriet Johnson Nursery School.

Harriet Johnson's interest in starting a school for young children included, besides the social-economic problems of parents, two trends, both of which were in the early stages of development. The first is represented by experimental education; the second, by child research. She organized her nursery school as a laboratory for experimentation along both lines. Not only did she reconcile these two trends in her work; she made each function more fully because of the other. Theoretically, this should always be the case; but in practice one of these interests usually prevails, to the detriment, if not the obliteration, of the other. Miss Johnson in 1916, was one of the three organizers of the Bureau of Educational Experiments and was continuously a member of its staff from then until her death. Although in its early years the Bureau was primarily an organization for child research, its psychological attitude toward research indicated an approach consistently educational as well as scientific.

This union of interests was rarer then than now. Many of the current battles that were being fought out in psychology and in biology had their reflections in the Bureau staff meetings. Miss Johnson both learned from and contributed to these discussions which defined the Bureau's research attitudes. The staff consistently regarded the child as an organic whole, thus joining the revolt against association psychology, welcoming in one field the newly stated Gestalt psychology and in another field the

study of behavior by C. M. Child and other workers in biology.

The Bureau's original interest in sequence of
growth in terms of maturity levels rather than of
age norms grew steadily with experience. From the
beginning the Bureau wished to study the relations
of the psychological and physical lines of development; so that much of its study concerned not only
records of sleep, nutritional condition, medical examination, and anthropometric measurement but
also systematic investigation of motor phases of behavior. The work of Arnold Gesell has since made
this attitude familiar. To mention only one more
attitude which jumps with the present trend in
child study, the Bureau always wished to study the
child in his natural setting. For that reason it chose
experimental schools as its laboratory.

Experimental schools were then in the early stage
of working out a curriculum based upon experience
rather than upon content. The more consistent of
them—a more accurate word than "radical"—were
attempting to make the school a laboratory where
children could make strategic discoveries about
things and people, a place where experience would
pass over readily and naturally into expression. The
Bureau group with whom Harriet Johnson worked
made a survey of twenty-seven of these early experimental schools in 1917, besides working in close
affiliation with the City and Country School, which
Miss Johnson always considered the original inspiration of her educational thinking.

Harriet Johnson had a genius for friendship and a genius for work. The two qualities were closely related. She understood the way other people thought and felt, and so could learn even from seemingly alien minds. This gift, combined with a singular integrity of purpose and thinking, enriched her own deep experiences. At the same time it kept her from the dogmatism, or "infallibility," which so often characterizes pioneer thinking. Thus she was able to apply the thinking of these experimental schools in a fresh way to the needs of younger children.

Miss Johnson's Nursery School was first organized by the Bureau of Educational Experiments in 1919* for children between the ages of fourteen months and four years. After nine years of experience as director, she published her book, "Children in the Nursery School," (John Day, 1928) which gives a full and graphic account of her principles and practice up to that time. Then followed six years in her nursery school where the range had been extended to cover the ages between two and six, and where were placed students from the Co-operative School for Student Teachers, a new Bureau venture. Thus came the challenging problem of developing teachers for experimental schools. Through these years the records of her work and her thinking appear in published articles; in accounts of talks delivered to educational conferences

* Before this she had worked as adviser to a small nursery school started by neighborhood mothers.

and to other interested groups, such as parents; and in notes used for planning work with the student teachers. Before she died, Miss Johnson had made a sizable start on writing out, in form for a proposed book, the digest of these years' experiences. This work was left unfinished. Part I of the volume in hand is comprised of this unfinished manuscript. Part II has been compiled from additional unpublished material and from excerpts from certain of her more recent published writings. Part III consists of typical records which she took of individual children, and of the studies she made from these records. The whole book has been planned to bring out those working ideas which seemed to be most important to her, and which most clearly marked her individual contribution to education. To this end there is a brief explanatory statement introducing each section.

Miss Johnson approached the problem of a nursery school with the educational viewpoint of working out an environment suited to the growth needs of two- and three-year-olds; and from the scientific viewpoint of recording and studying the children's behavior and analyzing their physiological and psychological development. She was singularly fitted by training and temperament to understand the wide gamut of these needs. She knew the physical needs of small children as a specialist knows them, and paid meticulous care to diet, sleep, and routine physical habits, sending a report home with each child each day to each mother. She was keenly alive to the emotional needs of these small human beings just emerging from complete dependence upon adults, still needing the security of affection to return to after valiant excursions into independence. She believed that these babies needed a warm relationship with the adults in the school, and was never afraid to be a human being—friendly, humorous, and responsive. She treated play, even in its earliest sensuous and motor manifestations, as an educational adventure, not as a "pre-educational" period to be outgrown as soon as possible. She recognized the educational play element in the children's motor experiments with their bodies, in the design quality in their block building, and in the rhythmic and colorful laryngeal activity which permeated their early language and often carried on its existence independently of content.

The problem of the school set-up—its equipment and program and the attitudes of its teachers—thus became quite literally the problem of constantly adjusting the environment to meet the physical, emotional, and intellectual needs of children of eighteen months, of two or three years, and later of four and five years. This meant thinking currently in terms of growth needs and of corresponding maturity levels.

Such a statement will sound fairly obvious to many people now. That this point of view within a nursery school no longer seems strange is due in no small measure to Harriet Johnson herself—to the influence of her writings and of her own nursery school. For she did not rest content with "hunches" as to maturity levels or with general impressions as to the success or failure of her nursery equipment; she felt it important to know how such behavior as food dislikes or control of urination was affected by the attitudes of the adults; she was interested in establishing any relationship that existed between a child's behavior and his physiological maturity as indicated by bodily proportions, use of small muscles, or method of going up or down stairs. She demanded of herself that the procedures within the nursery, even when based on hunches, be intentional to the point of being articulated; and that the results be recorded in terms of behavior and analyzed in terms of growth.

"Behavior norm," "motor pattern," "maturity level" were new expressions in nursery school language when she began to work out her behavior records. In addition to taking a full-day record of each child once a month, she and her staff lived with pencil and pad in their pockets, prepared for running comments. These records, even uninterpreted, make a genuine contribution to the methods of studying growth. They were not worked out in isolation; they bear the imprint of many minds. For seventeen years Miss Johnson worked with the specialists on the Bureau staff—physician, social worker, anthropologist, statistician, psychologist, and other special recorders. She was a member of the research staff as well as being director of the Nursery School, and her records provided the chief data for many purely research workers. Because of her rare ability to project herself into the thinking of other people, she probably profited by this "cooperative thinking" more than any other member of the group. She learned to speak their language, not quite as did the specialists themselves, but in a way which immensely enriched her own observational and interpretive powers. Some of her studies of individual children made from her long, full-day individual records over consecutive years, supplemented by the child's brief daily record and by a record of the activities of the whole group, are included in Part III of this book as a contribution to methods of study as well as to child psychology.

In the course of this discipline of record taking, Miss Johnson faced questions such as the technical reliability of her records; the value of qualitative descriptions of behavior which could not be reduced to quantitative measurements; the significance in understanding nursery school children of formal psychological tests, of bodily proportions, of home attitudes; and above all, the possibility of building the observations of the various specialists into an organic picture of a growing child. At the same time she was facing within the classroom such questions as: When should a child be given responsibility for his own actions, and when should the teacher take it for him? Is there a "pre-social" stage in which children react to one another in much the same experimental way that they do to things? What effect has emotional stability upon the development of work habits? And many, many more.

She came through to working answers on many of these fundamental problems of studying behavior and of interpreting behavior in terms of growth—of maturity levels. Some of these answers she embodied in her publications, some of them in the practices of her Nursery School, and some in her teaching at the Cooperative School for Student Teachers, of which she was so vital a part. But upon some she was still hard at work in February, 1934. That more of her thinking did not get into publication constitutes a major loss both to education and to child research. We hope, through this book, to mitigate that loss.

Enough of her thinking got into practice and into print to affect deeply the trend of nursery school development. There is still the danger of haphazard living in a nursery classroom, content with pleasant unchallenging "busy work," or with overstimulating or over-mature content. There is still the danger of losing the human relationship with little children in an attempt to assume the masklike impersonality of science; and the danger of basing the study of behavior upon situations which can be split into units and counted, regardless of the impulses behind the behavior or of the significance of conditioning factors. All of us know many nursery schools and much research work of these types. Harriet Johnson threw the weight of her experience against divorcing education and the study of growth, against recording children's behavior except in an educational environment, and against leaving an educational experiment unchecked by records. The extent of this contribution, the extent to which it is embodied in the nursery school which now bears her name and in the training school which she helped to organize, the extent to which it has permeated and modified the thinking of educators and research workers, present and future, cannot be measured. The contribution of pioneers is often absorbed into the work in its later stages of development. Perhaps that is a tribute to its worth.

Harriet Johnson made a unique contribution to the thinking of those of us who have compiled and edited the manuscripts in this book, her co-workers in the Bureau of Educational Experiments and in the Nursery School. Working over these papers, we have once more realized vividly the profundity of her philosophy, the exactitude of her methods, and the humanity of her approach to children. We are the richer for this work on Harriet Johnson's manuscripts. To her memory we present this gift to the educational world.

BARBARA BIBER
LUCY S. MITCHELL
JESSIE STANTON
LOUISE WOODCOCK

Bureau of Educational Experiments,
69 Bank Street,
New York City.

May 1, 1936

# PART I

Preschool Curriculum

*Adapting to School Experiences*
*The Functions of Play Activity*
*The Need for Selective Teaching*

## EDITORIAL NOTE

BEFORE her death Harriet Johnson had completed the first section of a book which was planned to cover the theory and practice of preschool education. This unfinished manuscript, because of its original purpose, surveys broadly certain key ideas which she undoubtedly intended to develop in terms of specific techniques in the later sections of the book. As it stands, it is neither a generalized discussion of an educational philosophy nor a manual of nursery school practice. It is, as anyone who had worked with Harriet Johnson would expect, an amazing integration of both. She had the technician's interest in the last detail; she had the philosopher's interest in ultimate significance; and her discussion of moot problems in the education of young children reveals this breadth of interest.

Her unfinished manuscript constitutes the following first section of this book, bringing to the fore such problems as: what the child must feel about the strangeness of school when he first encounters it; the ways in which home and school can and cannot meet on common ground; when and why we should expect our children to take on the customs of our social behavior; what the difference is between adapting to the regular routines of eating and sleeping and conforming to them; the teacher's role in establishing group equilibrium without the sacrifice of individual needs; the variety of functions served by an active play life; children's dramatization as a dy-

3

namic medium of expression; and finally, the figures of child and teacher considered in terms of the demands of the world beyond the school.

Obviously, such questions as these cannot be raised and discussed without sketching in a point of view. The reader who reads between the lines cannot fail to observe that Harriet Johnson, in the section which follows, has minced no words in her opposition to the outworn school of thought which would discipline the child, and is as clear in her rejection of that school of neo-discipline which would train the child to a premature efficiency and conformity. It may not be so clear to the reader, however, how far Harriet Johnson was ready to swing with the educational pendulum which moved for some years toward considering as most enlightened that brand of education which gave the whole rope to the impulses of the child's innermost nature. In this connection, her co-workers regret that she did not elaborate more fully her remarks on the emotional factors involved in the total configuration of child-in-school. The editor has taken the liberty to supply footnotes at those points where Miss Johnson's statements seemed too brief or too abrupt to represent the effort she was making at the time of her writing to untangle one of the knottiest problems in child education,—namely, the balance between the fulfillment of individuality and its adaptation to the prescribed way of living which human society requires.

## PRESCHOOL CURRICULUM

What do we mean by curriculum in the preschool groups? Reference to the nearest dictionary, an ancient Webster's Unabridged, gives us as its first meaning, "a race course; a place for running." Though this does not completely cover the subject, we could use it quite aptly from two years through six; but this definition is not the one we should choose. The second, "a specified, fixed course of study, as in a university," is disconcerting. It is as remote from our conception of the subject as the first, and more preposterous.

What, then, is our definition? Why do we think there is any more discussion needed about these early childhood experiences in school, beyond what has already been said about environment, play materials, activities, social interests and habit forming? Is it, perhaps, because environment planning in the schools of which we are writing is done with specific provisions in mind, beyond and besides those necessary for health; because play materials are selected rather than collected; and because environment and materials are planned quite frankly to encourage certain attitudes on the part of children, to build up certain interests, and to develop certain habits?

Whatever meaning the dictionaries give for curriculum, there is implied an intentional definite plan, which presumably has the backing of matured opinions and attitudes, and which involves a degree of limitation of materials, activities, and experiences; though it may also mean an extension of them. Above all, it presupposes an ordered analysis of observed behavior; the outlining of stages and phases in development; and the conception of certain interests and impulses dominant in early childhood, and of the steps in their development. It must also assume a logical relationship between the trends in behavior and the educational process, but a more subtle and intentional relationship than existed in the early years of nursery school experimentation.

Then, because adults saw children running, they gave them space to run; because they saw them absorbed in fitting objects into spaces, they provided peg boards; but they did not raise the question: is running invariably appropriate, everywhere and all the time? Can an activity like sticking things in holes develop with the developing powers of a child? In other words, are all the spontaneous activities of a child, even in an environment wisely planned for him, equally beneficial and valuable in growth?

Once raised, the question must be answered in terms of teaching skill and method. The emotional and the intellectual development of children, as correlates of physiological maturing, must guide the teacher in her choice of emphasis, her selection of which sign posts she will follow and which she will disregard.

Beyond all the knowledge she has built up of the steps in development, beyond all the skill she has acquired, there is a further step to be taken, and that the most daring. She must venture to declare her hypothetical answer to the main question at issue: what is an educated person? She will not answer in terms of subject matter. She will give us no categories; but she must know the attitudes, interests, and capacities she believes it desirable to foster, why she considers them important, and by what methods she proposes to further their development among the children in her care. In her answer, if she succeeds in being sufficiently explicit, we shall find a statement of curriculum for the preschool years.

## ADAPTING TO SCHOOL EXPERIENCES

Going to school for the first time at the age of two is an emotional hurdle which can not be ignored. It may take some adjusting even at four or five. Home has been life, and life has been home. Even if there have been excursions out of it, the stopping places have had no permanence. There has been no assumption that their qualities were those of home, no hint of belonging about them. Also someone from home was usually along; and home habits and home conventions were observed.

School is different. One finds that it has come to stay. It challenges one to a kind of effort and activity and experience that home may, indeed, have held, but which was incidental there. School lures, and it defeats. It delights and confounds. It is a magic place of small-sized chairs and tables in quantities; of small-sized persons, too; of many things which bid one touch and handle, tote and climb upon. Prohibitions at first seem nonexistent, the opportunity to do goes so far beyond the warning not to do. But even prohibitions may be precious, linking one surely to family adults. There are big people as well as small ones at school, but one can do one's small stunts, exhibit one's small prowess, give voice to one's pitiful lamentations or one's pigmy anger or protest, and win thereby only a return so inadequate in terms of adult concentration and concern, that this new world seems a strange and uncertain place. Sometimes the lure and enchantment win; sometimes the strangeness and the bigness are overwhelming, and all one can do is to adopt a mother-surrogate and cling with the desperation of the lost to the one feature of the landscape that has a hint of the familiar.

In the face of the usual acceptance of school and its ways with a modicum of reluctance and unhappiness on the part of children of all ages, the picture drawn above seems and is a gross exaggeration. However, I believe that in the majority of cases these emotional factors are present. The difference is that the tenseness is relieved and a prompt adjustment made possible by the steps the school takes to introduce children gradually to the new environment; by the skill of the teacher in standing in the place of the mother for the brief moments of strangeness; and by the capacity which resides in nearly all children to be wholeheartedly interested in their own concerns, to pursue them with an intense absorption, and to enjoy independence when once it is won. In the unstable or the unfortunately conditioned child we may find all these factors in active operation, generally for a fairly brief time. We cannot afford to be unaware that a process of adaptation is going on which, from the point of view of emotional stability, is one of the crises in development. This is true, whether it is accomplished painlessly or at great emotional expense.

It is obvious that school and home are equally important in education. The school environment is not the only one in which children are growing, carrying on activities, cultivating attitudes and prejudices and habits, and acquiring skills and information. Life would be less rich if this were so, and it would be unfortunate if home duplicated school or school duplicated home.

School must be a more objective and detached place, and home should be warmer and more glowing in its personal satisfactions. It is right that home should give a peculiar sense of belonging and of being essential and important. Its satisfactions have a quality different from those of school, where being one of a group, carrying out uninterruptedly one's own schemes of play, and feeling that one is an independent being, only make more keen the joys of withdrawal into the close family circle.

So far as either school or home has developed and can maintain an atmosphere in which the emotional life of the children can be freely flowing, buoyant, stable, and satisfying, their likeness is desirable; and if children can find the two consistent, the advantages of each are multiplied.

If the educational thesis on which the school is operating is sound, the more the home can share it, the more truly will its children be educated, the more fully will they live. It also follows that the rhythmic swing from the familiar and known out to the unfamiliar and back again will more easily be accepted as a pleasing variation, and fewer emotional conflicts will arise.

We know little about the inner urges and drives of little children. Despite current investigations of the inner life of the young, our available material still comes largely from the study of adult motivation, which leads us back by indirection to earlier urges. However, we must believe that overt behavior is not the whole story; that there are deep springs beneath, seeking outlet; and that normal living depends upon their finding natural channels or contributing their flow to the more placid streams of conscious conduct.

Our task as teachers is to shape our procedure so that school life will be as full and satisfying as possible. This means, first of all, to give children the sense of belonging. All of us are familiar with the violent affective response which babies make when the support on which they are resting is suddenly removed. Pressing an analogy, that is what happens spiritually when hours at school replace hours at home: security is disturbed.

There is a further assumption on which the teacher

proceeds: namely, that the process of maturing is as important as the goal reached. That is, if it were possible to cut the Gordian knot of adjustment to school, perhaps we should rob children of the valuable sense of self-direction and development. As far as we can see, acting his age is more satisfying to a healthy individual than being a baby. Being a baby, at any level, is a retreat; but being equal to taking an appropriate step in a given situation, whether it means leaving mother in the lower hall of the school and climbing alone to the play roof, or accepting a subordinate place in a social group, adds something to one's emotional stature.

Furthermore, one of the aims in this educational scheme, as far as it can be cramped into a statement, is to develop thinking capacity: to encourage an ability to look for relationships between events and processes. A child begins this search as soon as he begins to observe. He expresses it verbally before he has mastered elaborate language forms, by word sentences and word questions.

If he is crudely conditioned to required modes of behavior, he is motivated by something external to himself. If, on the other hand, his interests and his intelligence can be the sources of his adjustment to an active social community, he is understanding as he goes, up to the limits of his ability, whatever his age.

What does this mean in terms of teacher responsibility and of teacher-child relationship? First the teacher must establish herself as a person to be trusted: as a mother substitute in the sense of being relied upon, referred to, and permanent; and further, as reasonable competent authority, to be reckoned with in times of stress or doubt, when the child's peers prove inadequate. Then there must be constantly operative an intention on the teacher's part that dependence upon her must shift as speedily as may be to self-dependence on the part of the child. Till he feels both assured and free, till he has a relationship with the teacher that is genuine, he is not on sure ground.

Keeping faith with a child does not mean consoling or indulging him. It may mean a sharp, crisp prohibition; it may mean a removal of control from his hands to those of the adult; it may mean deprivation of a toy or a privilege; it may mean temporary banishment from the group, if community harmony is at stake.

If action of this sort is to be taken, it must be done with as much conviction and assurance as accompanies the welcoming, encouraging, inviting attitudes that have given children the freedom of the city. After the issue has been met, there must be no residue of blame or ill feeling left in the teacher's reaction. In fact, she must not only show no left-over blame: she must feel none. She must be able to tolerate a child whose response to a situation cannot be tolerated for a moment. She acts; but the child's position in respect to her remains the same, and after he has realized that his act is not acceptable and that repetition of it carries a penalty, he finds himself on the same footing as before. The teacher has kept faith.

Teacher interference with children's activity is usually called for in situations involving the group; which brings us to another statement of policy. We are not taking as our goal the preparation of children for easy conformity to society as we find it. We are frankly trying to establish in our school environment a community in which fair play prevails; in which the materials belong to all and must be shared; in which possession is established only by use; in which construction is encouraged, and destruction and attack not permitted, whether directed toward animate or inanimate objects; in which emphasis is put on good sportsmanship and a friendly relationship with one's peers. Little by little a better way than brute force is demonstrated as a social technique: the request for a toy, rather than the strong arm method; observance of turns, instead of scrambling to get in ahead; respect for others' activities and constructions, instead of ruthless interruption and destruction.

Vigor is not sacrificed by this method; for though the fangs of ruthlessness are at long last drawn, there are occasions that call for sturdy resistance, there are opportunities for friendly wrestling among the children and for active assertion of one's rights. After the general tenets of the commonwealth are accepted, close adult supervision and direction lapse, and the children route themselves through the ordinary day's program with quite remarkable independence and accord.

Some of these children will meet the social code of the street. Some will find an insistence upon the practice of adult social conventions. As the teacher watches children together, she finds an almost universal responsiveness to justice and fair play, and realizes that the social practices and attitudes which have become current among her group would have values in any society. Children seem able to establish an understanding with each other by some technique more subtle (perhaps because more simple) than adults' cumbersome methods. We have woven into our social relationships such a web of tradition, of convention, of inhibition, that we rarely make at once a true social contact with a person or group we are meeting for the first time. We are more primitive than a child. We revert to neolithic caution. We do not quite raise our hackles, but we do the modern equivalent. We are affected by small considerations of appearance, language, race, familiarity, acceptance and use of the particular mores current in the circles we know best. We keep ourselves back to a far greater extent than children would if their social life could begin before society had fastened its tentacles into them. At least in the school group we try for simplicity and directness, hoping that there may be a carry-over into later social attitudes.

Another demand that society makes upon the young is acquaintance with the conventional forms which obtain among civil adults, and an appropriate use of them. We believe that Dr. Gesell's statement that "training cannot transcend maturation" is particularly relevant, when we come to determine just what shall be our policy in regard to the moot question of manners.

Exposure to civility and to its verbal expression is important. The habits of persons most closely associated with children are taken over by them as they reach the age of susceptibility to one and then another particular virus. If we could make a study of the point at which the human organism becomes aware of the different conventional forms and capable of adopting them as modes of behavior, I believe we should find that greetings and "please" and "thank you" come fairly early; that "excuse me" and "you are welcome" come distinctly later; and that going between two persons who are talking, and speaking out of turn, are not felt as social errors till well into adolescence, unless they are accompanied by penalties unfailing and severe. Similarly I think that the nuances of table manners—the treatment of one's implements, waiting for everyone to be served, not choosing the choicest, or rather the largest, serving—are entirely lost upon children till the adolescent awareness of themselves makes them look at other people and desire to be so like them that they shall avoid being conspicuous.

This does not mean that we should not, long before this time, acquaint children with these forms and, after early childhood, insist upon the observance of many of them, especially those which have a real social value. But it is much more important in the interest of courtesy that children acquire a kind of friendly attitude, which gives and expects fair play and no malice. The first thing to learn in social relationships is to live and let live, and it takes a deal of learning. The next is to respect the rights of other persons.

When a two-year-old looks at the ball in the hands of another child, and goes to a shelf to get one for himself instead of appropriating the more obvious and ready one, he has begun to respect, if not to understand, certain social traditions. When a four-year-old drops to his knees to rebuild a block structure which he has inadvertently knocked down in passing, he has recognized a social responsibility and has made the gracious disarming gesture which is more effective and universally understood than a verbal apology.

Perhaps if expressions of courteous consideration came to the lips of adults as often as prohibitions and reproofs, our children would become habituated to them as they are to other adult forms which they use before they entirely comprehend them. In any case, any more direct coaching than that of scrupulous use of them by the teachers seems fruitless labor. As to the intricacies of table etiquette, emphasis upon it seems to me a shocking waste of children's time and a serious threat to good appetite and good digestion.

Freedom of choice in play activities is a nursery school slogan; but in the interest of health and of general satisfaction and serenity the routine features of the program remain in the teacher's hands. Meal time, washing time, resting time, picking-up time, are announced according to schedule, and enough in advance so that they will interrupt as little as possible the activities in progress. Compliance is taken for granted, and for the most part these routines are accepted without question. They are found to be as inevitable as day and night, and adult authority in regard to them is immutable. Reluctances carried over from home, or the early resistance to intimate personal routine in a strange setting, may interfere sometimes with a prompt response to all details. However, no choice is given; there is little discussion; and adults show no emotional response over children's failures to eat or sleep, or their objections to other details. If a child's difficulties become disturbing to the group, he may not remain in it; but on the whole, the performance of routine parts of the program raises less comment or apparent interest from the teachers than play activities.

The first attitude that is taken in regard to eating and sleeping is one of non-interference. To illustrate with the youngest children: in some cases appetite is so keen that it downs all other emotions; and where one's table is set, and whether the ritual is always the same, matter not. In others the breaking of bread is distinctly a home ceremony, and there may be complete refusal to eat, or appetite may be materially lessened. Whatever the child's attitude, no pressure is put upon him. He receives a moderate portion, and is fed, if that method proves acceptable. After the plate has been before him for a time, it is removed; and dessert, then milk, is served him. A casual comment may be made, that everyone eats dinner here, or that help will be given if he wishes; but there is no attempt to force the situation. As the days pass, the feeling of easy familiarity, of acquaintance and belonging, eases strain; and the hours of active play out-of-doors stimulate appetite, so that sober, solemn attention to the business in hand, with a resulting clean plate, makes dinner time in the two-year-old group an impressive exhibition.

This is a picture of it at its best. After the initial adjustment there remain the poor eaters, children who, with no positive physical defects, and in spite of favorable hygienic conditions, continue to have only moderate appetites; and there may be children whose aversion to certain foods is so pronounced that special techniques must be used. With these youngest children, even serious food problems can be solved as experience in the group builds up confidence in adults, the sense that each event in the school day holds its own delights, knowledge that the expression of likes and dislikes will rouse no alarm, and furthermore the realization that if one really does not eat, one goes to bed while the group of feasters is still crunching delectable toast or gorging applesauce.

Etiquette at this stage consists in an occasional warning about spilling and about spoons that are loaded too heavily for effective service. Toast is not soaked, and milk cups are not used as finger bowls. Your strong teeth can bite the toast. You drink the milk; and if it is in the way, it can go away till you are ready for it. The solemnity of the early weeks gives way, as social awareness wakens, to a roistering spirit, which appears after the first edge of appetite is satisfied.

Adults have charge of serving, so there is no occasion for the children to leave their tables. Certain individuals are likely to do so, however, and any excuse will serve them. It is noticed as little as possible, but they are reseated promptly and often asked if they have finished eating and are ready for bed. A persistently restless child may find himself detained in his chair by a wide soft sash, applied as a help to dining comfortably, not in a disciplinary manner. This may seem a drastic measure; but offered, as it is, casually and as an assistance rather than as a punishment, it is usually accepted and sometimes called for. When there is objection, it is not used; but the reminder is given that it is now eating time. It is a debatable question whether a child so young should be expected to sit at table throughout a meal without a change. Unless he actually leaves his chair he is not reminded of his position. He is pulled back if he slumps, his legs are removed from the top of his table, and his attention is called back to feeding by the adult's giving him a spoonful or placing his spoon in his hand.

Violent kicking and scuffing are very contagious and distracting forms of dinner entertainment. Removal of shoes is the only corrective given, and for some occult reason the inquiry if shoes need to come off is enough to still the most persistent scuffer.

No issues are raised. The argument that children need to face issues is sometimes brought up in regard to such techniques. True enough, but the issue here is that of learning to eat a meal in which a variety of foods is served in a place which is not home: to eat and to enjoy eating, and to feel as little restraint as possible. In short, the standards that are set up are such that immaturity can accept them, and the "learning situation" that the teacher has in mind is the anticipation and enjoyment of good food in good company.

The question of sitting quietly at table, of attending to the business of eating and of not disturbing other children, can be met more directly in the three- to four-year-old group. Here again, and in fact throughout the school, eating what one finds on one's plate is treated as a matter of course. We all eat everything, even if we do not like it very well.

Three-year-olds may be fed, if the meal drags and feeding helps. It is a long process for the slow child; and food grows less and less palatable, the longer it is left on a plate. Also, companionship adds zest to dining; a bit of conversation with a teacher makes the last few remnants of the main course slip down, and dessert can generally carry itself.

Toast and dessert come after dinner is finished; and the assumption is that you are not hungry enough to need these delicacies if you still have food on your plate. As a rule it seems to me to be questionable policy to put a premium on sweets and make them the goal of dinner; but when they are as innocuous as dried bread and stewed fruit, it appears to be a mild indulgence. At all events, this rule obtains from two through five and does help to speed up laggards.

Over the entire age range our policy is one not of forcing compliance with given standards but of maintaining an atmosphere of interest and cooperation. Likes and dislikes are recognized by the time we are five, but we always eat a little of things that we do not like. We learn to like certain things and are quite proud of it.

There is not perfect order at our tables. At four and five there is much conversation hardly worthy of the name, so much of it is rank nonsense. There are experimental sallies: vain attempts to leave food and get by. There is a very crude use of table utensils, and some misuse on the part of the more excitable diners.

The teacher's aim is to get this business of feeding reduced to pleasant and fairly orderly terms, to make dinner a happy occasion, and gradually to introduce habits that bring the children's performance nearer the standard that can satisfy adults, rather than to enforce these social conventions by continued attention to them.

There is a vital distinction between asking a child to conform to standards and situations, and asking him to adapt to them. Adaptation involves him in a more active self-determined process, in which he and the situation are mutually engaged. The process of adaptation is going on constantly as he establishes himself in the school community, responds to school conditions, and makes use of school materials. There is interaction as well as action going on. In the case of the routine activities, I should say that we require conformity to the time program but that we try to leave room for a gradual adaptation to social forms. Habits which are objectionable or disturbing, like messing with food or beating upon the table, are corrected, but with the reminder that it is time to eat and that such behavior disturbs the others at table, rather than that it is not good form. In other words, the reminders and explanations are put, as far as possible, upon a level which the child will comprehend, rather than upon one which is of no interest and no concern to him, and to which he does not really attend. In this latter case it is the adult's domination of the situation that affects him, not the desirability or the reasonableness of the requirement.

Positive but casual approval is given to good techniques, such as keeping a tidy table or efficiently disposing of food without recourse to fingers; but the approval is given quietly to the individual in question, not of him to the group.

The same policy obtains in regard to resting and nap. There is an effort to make conditions such that adult direction is at a minimum. As far as possible, the youngest children have individual sleeping quarters. We try to devise mechanical aids to quiet, instead of making a direct appeal to a child. For instance, if he sits up in bed or rolls about restlessly, his sleeping bag is pinned at the corners so that his movements are somewhat restricted. This procedure becomes routine, and adults are reminded by the child if they omit the pins. If he is noisy and keeps himself awake by talking or calling, he is usually given another crib where there will be less to distract him. The reminder that another child nearby has gone to sleep seems to quiet some individuals for the moment, till they are themselves overcome.

As the children get older, a more direct appeal can be made. Fours and fives are reminded to lie quietly, to get into comfortable positions, and then to be as still as possible. Attempts to disturb other children are treated as is most other anti-social conduct, by withdrawal from the group. Thus in group situations as well as in individual ones we attempt to give the child opportunities to adapt in his own way, as far as possible, so that the springs of action will remain his own, not external to him in the power of the adult to dominate him. Domination by the adult is necessary on occasion, but if our objective is to entrust more and more power to a child, to let him find his own methods of control as long as they are workable, the occasions for autocratic interference will be progressively fewer, and a common source of emotional conflict will be reduced.

Health habits and the physical examination are treated from a similar point of view. It is assumed that one eats because one is hungry and the food is good, not because of the vitamin content or in order to grow. The doctor is going to see how fine one is, not if one is well. From the adult standpoint the school examination is valuable because it establishes the physician as another pleasant adult acquaintance. It gradually breaks down reluctances which may have been built up by unfortunate but unavoidable associations during illness, associations with pain or fear. We also regard it as one of our best instruments for parental education. The examination looks not mainly to the correction of pronounced defects but to the assessment of the child's equipment and the means by which it may be made more adequate for use. This is coming to be more and more the practice of the modern pediatrician; but too often parents call a physician only in cases of acute illness, letting minor but serious deviations from the highest standards of functions go unnoticed. Giving the parents a demonstration of what a really thorough physical examination should be illustrates for them the importance of details of development and often raises their standard of health.

The child is not present at the interview between parent and physician, and criticism of weight, posture, or carriage, or of defects or remedies, is avoided. General ideas of good and bad health are irrevelant topics of discussion for the young child, irrelevant because the kind of awareness and understanding he has are under the control of less abstract interests, and because, fundamentally, such ideas do not engage his feelings.

The emotions he expresses are largely a product of

sensations, those sensations that concern himself and his person. This remains true even while we realize that there is an uncontrolled and unconscious emotional motivation affecting all behavior, and constituting the source of personality development. The observable flow of direct emotional expression does not universally derive from the deeper springs of feeling, but may in some instances be grafted on, as other tricks of manner are.

If a child is hurt, he cries; if he is thwarted, he shows anger; his physical activities and social contacts give him pleasure, and he laughs; but at two and three he is oblivious of future states, and at four and five the future he visions is one which concerns him and his activities and is usually similar to something that has already come to pass. The three-year-old can say, "Mama spank me, I get out my bed a-night"; but that apparent understanding deters him no whit from repeating his misdemeanor. The four-year-old announces that mother is going to take her to the zoo if she has a nap, but the anticipation cannot restrain her from her usual restlessness, and she is genuinely dismayed when the promised excursion is postponed. That is, all we get is a parroting of our words, on subjects into which the inexperience and immaturity of our children make it impossible for them to enter with genuine understanding.

The older the child, the wider the range of pseudo-emotional tinges one finds in his responses. Petty forms of resentment, jealousy, revenge, malice, preferences for one person and exclusion of another, such as we are familiar with in the adult, appear frequently and make one realize how immature much adult conduct is; and by the ebb and flow and change of this childish behavior, we are shown, too, how superficial is the basis of much of it in the child.*

The skillful teacher treats humorously some of these manifestations, and diverts attention from others while she suggests an occupation which will fully engage the physical powers of the disgruntled or injured individual. She may say that so-and-so would make a fine ticket collector, if an indignant boat captain has refused to take him on as a passenger. She will see that two children who are conspiring against the others are routed by separate paths during most of their occupations and that they each make other contacts that bring them satisfaction. "Oh, we all like everybody here," as a casual response to a "We don't like him" chorus, gets to be a substitute slogan; and though it means as little as the other to the chanting choir, it makes for harmony. In other words, the teacher regards many of the expressions used by chil-

* In the editor's opinion, the above remarks indicate that Miss Johnson was intent on discovering, through direct observation, what childish reactions express truly deep emotion and in which instances behavior which resembles emotional expression really represents something less. She was aware, as the material suggests, of the vital factor of the affective phase of development. Here, as elsewhere, she applied the principle of estimating a child's behavior in terms of its predominant trends. Because of this it seemed essential to her to take into account the transitory nature of certain emotional expressions in the everyday life of children, and consequently to avoid the error of putting too much interpretative weight upon isolated items of behavior.

dren as being imitative rather than as originating in true feeling, as drama rather than as emotion; and she treats them accordingly, with a light touch.

In order that her role shall not be solely one of correction, she will watch the signs of the times and prevent conflict, whenever possible, instead of letting the repeated performance establish a pattern. Above all, she will try to find out why the child's responses have taken this anti-social turn, what experiences he has met that have taught him these techniques, for what impulse he is seeking satisfaction by conduct that brings him into unpleasant relationship with other children and with adults as well.

Unfriendly attacks and interferences, and behavior that persistently annoys other children, need checking; and there must be no doubt in the mind of the aggressor that authority rests with the adult. Certainty in regard to the teacher and her place in the scheme of things is as necessary for the children's serenity as the other conviction that school is their own place. It is this certainty that children rest upon. It frees them for attention to their legitimate concerns and leaves the teacher no less a trusted friend. A fearful person cannot give them this assurance. The teacher who really regards children as persons with whom she has a genuine relationship can approach this matter of discipline with decision. She will recognize that she is the senior partner in the cooperative enterprise of the school program, and she will assume without hesitation authority for as much of the children's behavior as they are not yet mature enough to control without help.*

Such is the teacher's thesis regarding preschool education. On these conclusions she bases her program, which is to be differentiated sharply from the daily schedule. Program signifies the opportunities which the school offers children intentionally throughout a year, the method by which the school makes sure that these opportunities will be used, and the variations in experiences and methods that are introduced as the children grow in maturity.

Opportunities are given which introduce children to the physical environment; establish them in their social group; and orient them in regard to the school as a whole, to their own place in it, and to the activities going on there. Very important also are opportunities which offer a means of expression. These

---

* It is a matter of regret to Miss Johnson's colleagues that she did not elaborate more fully in this connection the teacher's responsibility for sensing the individual child's needs. Had there been opportunity to complete her unfinished writing, there is little doubt that she would have given serious and detailed attention to this important problem. In so far as the above remarks refer to techniques, these are much more a setting of the stage than a laying down of rules. The teacher is expected to be a factor in maintaining a positive atmosphere in the school situation taken as a whole. This does not preclude her giving leeway to negative expression on the part of individual children whenever and to the degree to which she judges it necessary to the child and permissible within a group situation. The psychological security which the children gain from the teacher's willingness to assume the responsibility of control is a point more familiar to educators and psychologists now than it was at the time of Miss Johnson's writing, only two years ago.

will be accepted and used by each individual to an extent depending on how far the teacher's enlightenment and wisdom have enabled her to anticipate or find out individual needs. Our feet are on fairly solid ground when we work from observation of overt behavior back to play materials and to opportunities for experience and expression.

If we are really wise enough, we shall find the play and the language of even two- and three-year-old children revealing impulsive tendencies based on the deeper emotional levels. We know that the teacher's behavior, also her convictions, interests, emphases and objectives, derive from similar sources. What we are, what we believe, and how we act, are so thoroughly dependent upon our native endowment and upon how life has affected us in unknown, unrecognized ways as well as in those of which we are aware, that it is difficult to work out a philosophy based upon objective reasoning, not upon subjective rationalization.

It seems fairly certain that each individual is concerned in the development of his "style," the front he carries before the world. Quite without conscious intent he is building his affective structure. It may be one whose walls allow for free interchange between him and the world to which he has access and to which he must be making constant responses. It may grow to serve him solely for protection and defense, in which case, though it expresses him no less, it will bring him less satisfaction, a more meagre sense of fulfillment. It will stand between him and the process of integration, instead of aiding him in his growth as a social being.

Because of the complexity of the affective organization, it is probably true that all human beings build up a field of operations in which certain areas of sensitivity are bulwarked against invasion and certain limits of action are set. Within that field a majority of us live, with comparative satisfaction to ourselves and our fellows. In fact, the personality of an individual is thus formed by a series of genuine adjustments and readjustments, and is healthy in that the result is a capacity for active living.

### THE FUNCTIONS OF PLAY ACTIVITY

It is doubtless impossible to estimate just how far a rich play life enables children to live through and resolve the conflicts involved in the early processes of growing up.

There is sufficient similarity of impulsive behavior among all of the children known in the nursery school for the teacher to feel justified in regarding as characteristic certain needs of an inner emotional life. The expression of these needs suggests both an urge to establish a contact with the external world of people and things, and a desire to retain considerable fantasy content.

Little is known as yet, despite hypothetical conjectures, about the relation between fantasy interests and active play expression. We do not know to what extent play materials satisfy archaic inarticulate desires. We only know that they allow children to express meanings which need never be interpreted to or by adults; and also allow increasingly complex representation of experiences, which may or may not have double values.

I believe there is distinct danger in the teacher's attempting a more definitive role than is here implied. She needs to be aware of the complexity of the emotional life, but this will affect her method only in extending her range of values, in giving her the realization that a child's use of materials need not be circumscribed by the intention of the school program, and that there is no necessity for over-stressing that pedagogical fetish, production. In avoiding the pitfall of amateurish psychology she will still hold the function of teacher, which means that her policy must remain one of active relationship with her children and consideration of the growth needs which the school is planned to serve. The problem of the school is not how far and how fast an individual can mature, but by what impulses and through what interests children do mature and how their native resources, as aids to growth, can be used in the educational process.*

* In these passages Miss Johnson has touched on one of the crucial problems of current educational thinking and has outlined a position with respect to it. The position she takes, namely, that the teacher needs to understand how spontaneous play may serve the double function of helping the child to express deep emotional needs and to clarify the world of external relations, and that the role of teacher is to be defined primarily in terms of the latter (that is, of the child's relation to the external world) is one which finds strong current support in the writings of those who have lately attempted to correlate the psychiatrist's and the educator's understanding of growing children.

If we base our school planning on such investigations as these, we imply that there are certain tendencies which are common to children in early childhood; that there are age levels or, rather, developmental differences which can be explored; and further, that experiences offered children must have continuity as growth has continuity, and that in content and in challenge to interest they must be stimulating to further activity and an increase in power.

We believe that there are certain observable tendencies in children's play activities, which act as enzymes in their effect on development. First, there is the obvious impulse toward activity, toward the use of all muscular equipment. Primarily a self-protective race-inherited instinct, it serves development in a way that need not be argued. The steps from early random movements to locomotion, to seizing, grasping, and pulling, have been the subject of exhaustive study. Less has been said about the effect upon emotional and social development, and the result in satisfaction (itself a potent stabilizer in the growth of personality), of a sure control of the body in the variety of play situations in which one meets one's mates.

Recorded observations give repeated instances of irritation and disappointment shown at the inability to control muscles and make them answer the calls made upon them, and at inability through them to control the materials in the environment. Elation and satisfaction over physical accomplishments, and interest evidenced by repetition of a new process or feat, are equally common.

A two-year-old who had just stepped off a curb, for the first time, unsupported, repeated his performance till the observer lost count. A child of three announced her first real two-footed jump with a shout, "I did!" going back to jump over and over again. A four-year-old, making a block structure in which delicate balance was involved, screamed and scolded her neighbor when the building fell repeatedly. When she had met the problem successfully, she smiled, clapped her hands, and danced about.

Derived from activity and integrating it, are found the tendencies, first, to experiment with the motor skill, and to embroider the simple performance; and second, to follow it into an exploration and investigation of the environment.

It is an age-old observation that children do not leave their surroundings as they find them. They shift and change and adapt, frequently to no end but destruction, from the adult's point of view, and often for the sole purpose of exercising newly found powers.

The older theologues had a name for it. They called it Original Sin, and spelled it with capital letters. It remained for the modern pedagogue to see that it could be capitalized in another way. She calls it the beginnings of scientific inquiry, and gives the young inquirers a laboratory: the classrooms and playgrounds of the newer education. Here she provides selected play materials, taking as one of the

basic principles these tendencies which she has observed in children: the impulse to be active, to gain
control of the muscles in a variety of situations; to
explore and investigate the physical environment;
and to change it and adapt it to ends of their own.

Whichever age in early childhood she may be observing, she sees these impulses at work; but she notes
that the motor skills attained, and the end apparently
sought, vary progressively with age, so that the activities of two-year-olds differ so strikingly from
those of five-year-olds that they seem to be those of
two different species. The common factor of constant activity, investigation, and experimenting, runs
through both age groups; and the longer she watches,
the more she finds a constant dynamic swing or
rhythm in each, back toward the younger level and
out toward the older one.

Examining the effect upon the individual of increasing bodily skill, ingenuity, and power, she finds
that he has gained an amazing amount of information
about the physical features of his environment. At
first the things he met had their way with him. The
wagon decided what course he should pursue, defeating his purpose. The swing he pushed caught him
on the rebound and prostrated him, and he rose only
to be floored again. Even the older children did not
entirely escape this domination of physical things.
The climbing apparatus mocked their efforts, clay
refused to take the forms desired, and tools and
wood had to be learned before they could be used.

Gradually, by dint of a persistence which gives us

a hint as to profitable teaching methods, there is acquired a degree of power and understanding which gives these immature human beings mastery over their surroundings to the extent of their dealing with them. Again the desire for power, and its fulfillment, seem to have an integrative effect upon development. Emotional security is more firmly established, activity has direction, the child's relationship to his school life seems to have more organic reality.

What the teacher sees is renewed zest in play, purpose extending beyond muscle activity, an assurance in manner, and an increase in gaiety and overt expressions of satisfaction. She adds to the base on which she is building, another native impulse: to seek to gain power over the physical environment.

Another outstanding tendency that presents itself to the teacher's observation has to do with the social interest of children. The social obliviousness and lack of skill characteristic of very young children gradually gives way, through quite finely graded steps, first to an awareness of each other; then to greater dependence upon each other's presence; later as language grows more proficient, to a real give-and-take in playing together, which finally emerges into co-operative schemes of play, fairly well organized and sustained, involving shared responsibilities which are regarded with a certain degree of seriousness. Remarks about social understanding have to be made cautiously and with qualifications, for the swing of the pendulum back to early stages, noted in the case of motor activities, is even more characteristic of social maturing. Awareness of each other and desire for play contacts are fully awake by the age of three, but even at four a large percentage of time is spent in independent activities. At four and five language is not completely adequate to carry one's ideas unless they are of the simplest. When is it, for that matter? No other means of communication is so susceptible of misinterpretation.

On a chart which recorded week by week the types of social play observed in a two-year-old group, there was shown at first hardly more than a diffuse awareness, among the children, of each other's presence. Then came a distinct seeking not for actual contact but for proximity, leading to the choice of like types of play or material. Toward the end of the year there were closer contacts, more instances of sharing materials by mutual agreement, more language interchange, and more notice of each other in the form of inquiries about each other's occupations, directed at first to the teacher about a child, then directly to the child. At the luncheon hour, when the first children were taken through the room where the others were eating, to be put to bed, there were no group comments at all early in the year; but by February a child's appearance in a sleeping bag was always the signal for a full chorus of goodbyes.

Actual social play is fleeting at two; but from the time when the first realization dawns upon one that this other living, acting, moving being is not me but is like me, there is an impulse that increases steadily, an impulse to affect that being. The first attempt takes the form of doing to it just what one does to inanimate objects. Little by little one's methods become more subtle; language comes to one's aid; and finally, doing something by cooperative effort is proved to be the most effective instrument for gaining power over the social environment.

Here the much debated question of leadership arises. What capacities for leadership has a child from two to four or five years old? And with his capacities, what sort of leadership should we find him achieving?

If by leadership is meant the ability to dominate and control a situation so that things that are happening are interrupted, that people are disturbed and their activities checked or diverted, then no one is too young to qualify as a leader. Obviously, that is not what the term is meant to imply; though I have heard children referred to as leaders, whose effect upon a group was hardly more than that. True leadership is not a native quality. The potential capacity for it may be, and, I suspect, can be recognized early. Capacity and function are not synonymous, however; and both must be in active operation in the leader.

A leader must, first of all, have ideas and a plan, else where will he lead? He must, second, be able to communicate his plan, which involves some language facility. In the third place, he must be able to hold his followers and win their active cooperation, so that his scheme, which, if he is truly a leader, involves them in active participation, will take shape as he has planned it and come to some sort of fulfillment. He must have the gift of organization; and his ideas, through some appeal in his personality, must win enthusiasm from his mates.

A child may have any one of these traits and be a valuable member of a group without taking the position of leader. One five-year-old always contributed valuable ideas in the discussion period and was active in play, but failed to enlist the interest of his group in the play schemes which he carried out so well by himself. A four-year-old was able to attract her mates to activities which she originated, but her plans always reduced them to passive observers. A three-year-old had a ready imagination, and his dramatic play was full of content; but so much of his drama was dependent upon his own fantasy and imaginary props rather than upon actual materials, that the children who had joined him at first were soon left behind.

The mental spryness and the volubility of certain children may give them a fictitious place in a group; and the slow child who waits to take his cue from his more active fellows may, if his way is cleared and he is thrown upon his own initiative, develop an individual mode of expression which will deepen his satisfaction.

All this by way of saying that though we shall certainly find children who show the capacity for becoming outstanding figures in any group, our efforts can more effectively be directed to the development of each individual to his fullest capacity than to encouraging signs of leadership and giving selective opportunities to children who seem specially endowed. Gesell says that growth potency, the capacity for continued development, is probably the mark of individual superiority. While early maturing may be another sign, we still know very little about heredity and environment, about what traits are native and persist even under adverse conditions of nurture, and to what degree abilities can atrophy from disuse or turn themselves from beneficent to adverse influences through misuse. We see brilliant children failing of their promise, their talents turning upon their own personalities to wreck them. We see individuals of undistinguished intelligence using all their resources to such advantage that their lives have real dignity and bring rich satisfaction to themselves and others. Not only do we know little about the sources and significance of growth impulses, but we are only at the beginning of the study of their cultivation. We do not know, for instance, at what expense the abilities of the exceptional, able child are exploited when he is prematurely given the sense of power over his fellows: at what expense to his emotional stability and that of his fellows, who may appear quite ready to follow him and even to acknowledge his superiority by their attitudes toward him.

Even if our knowledge were more absolute and our methods more refined, the wisdom of training for leadership thus early would be open to question. Leaders are needed in adult communities, but quite as surely are there needed competent and intelligent cooperators, without whom leadership goes down to defeat. In children's groups a pooling of the resources of all the members, as far as possible, is the indicated procedure; and here the teacher has one of her most important and intricate problems.

One of the safeguards present, in the nature of things, in early childhood is children's absorption in individual play. It is a commonplace that two young children playing together do not have necessarily a common purpose. In a two-year-old group two children were observed, much absorbed in loading large blocks into a packing case. They were working in harmony, with no apparent difference of opinion. One was heard to say, as he dumped his load, "I'm a moving man." The other, with no reference to the first remarked, "This is my garage." Occasionally something like this obliviousness occurs at four; and even in what we call the cooperative play of five-year-olds, the part that each child takes gives him a good deal of leeway in interpreting his role and in developing side lines of activity.

In a complicated boat play observed in a five-year-old group, in which five children were engaged at one time, even the construction was being made by individuals or small groups with little reference to each other. Three of the children were making the dining saloon, another was busy at the captain's bridge and still another was arranging the gangplank. There was some communication among them and when the captain gave the "all aboard" signal there was response from all the children.

The fact that there is so little permanent unity in the social group makes it more possible for each child to develop his own ideas. The teacher will see that he has a chance to express them to the group if he wishes.

The impulse to affect the social environment, believed to be an impelling and significant one, may mean not a desire to dominate it but to count in it, to be felt in some measure within it. Teasing and interfering are methods developed by individuals who are unable in constructive ways to establish themselves in a group of their fellows. At the same time that such tendencies, which are inimical to the group integration, are checked, a substitute procedure must be offered; if possible, in such a way that it can compete in attractiveness with the anti-social behavior, which had, at least, the advantage of bringing its author into the limelight.

There is a subtlety in the techniques which the skillful teacher uses which baffles description. She has at the same time to maintain the integrity of her relationship with the children and to approach them on the level which they have reached. She will not say to three-year-old Tom, who has refused to divide the hoard of shovels he has collected, "You must share them with Jimmie;" but she may say, "Jimmie has no shovel, and there are none on the shelf. Which one are you going to give him?" If there are more on the shelf and Jimmie is in the stage of not seeing inert material not in use, and so is appropriating Tom's, she will not adjure him, "You must not take Tom's toys," but will say, with a hand outstretched for his, "Tom is using these. I'll show you where there are some more for you." If four-year-old Jack repulses Dorothy when she tries to get on board his train, no remarks about his social duties will change his feeling that he does not wish to play with Dorothy. But when the teacher gives her a piece of paper and says to Jack, "Here's a passenger for your train. She has her ticket. Where do you want her to sit?" the chances are that not only will Dorothy be accepted but that tickets and passengers also will be added to the play scheme.

These are not cited as invariable approaches. They are not magic and would not be acceptable in every case. They are brought up as illustrations of a method that tends to put children in a receptive rather than a negative mood, and which in the end will build up more profitable habits than a disciplinary procedure. The fact is that children for the most part live in a world in which they are dominated either by adults, by social conventions, or by the circumstances of their inferiority in strength, maturity, and judgment. Much of their negative behavior, their insistence, their unlovely resistant responses, arises not from considered reflection upon the injustices they feel but as a primitive reaction of the human organism to discomfort and lack of ease.

Resistance in one form or another is likely to continue as long as the vital interests of children are not given opportunity to thrive. The nursery school should offer such opportunity with as few adult-dictated interludes as possible, though with entire adult control. There must never be doubt as to where responsibility rests, and the authority of the teacher should be as unquestioned as it is welcome. A three-year-old "introduced" his teacher to a visitor, "There's a lady here, Miss Parker, wha' takes care of us." Taking care evidently meant to him something more than the attention to physical needs often given him by student assistants.

The desire to affect the social environment appears later than the desire to affect the physical environment but seems no less a characteristic interest of early childhood. Like the latter, it seeks a constructive outlet and is best served when the child is able to establish play relationships with his mates.

By constructive outlet is meant a play use of materials, or play with other children, that shows some organization, that calls upon past experience or learning, that adds something to the present enjoyment of the child or to his resources, and that has proved itself to be of biological significance. A weighty announcement like that seems to reduce play to the limbo of didactic training, and suggests that a preschool curriculum must be the invention of a medieval pedagogue. It must be remembered that play is considered quite seriously the most important concern of childhood; and that in a child's investigations of his environment the information he gathers is of no importance unless it stimulates and enlivens his

activities. By biological significance is meant, importance due to furthering the organic growth process,
the integration of personality development.

Play which calls upon past experience is characteristic of children from about eighteen or twenty
months on. It is so universal that this wise observant
teacher of ours adds what she calls dramatic play to
the list of dynamic impulses activating young children, and she provides for it in her school planning.

Perhaps it may seem to dignify it too much to call
the play we mean dramatic. It is mimetic surely, but
anything approaching literal imitation is far beyond
the powers of little children. The baby of eighteen
months who pranced up and down with a wagon for
a few steps and said, "I pony," recalled to himself
and the watching adult the real flavor of a lively
pony. The performance was part of his play of pulling a wagon, and perhaps prancing came first and
served as a reminder that ponies were other animals
that pranced and pulled wagons. At all events, it
evidently enhanced his enjoyment, for his chuckles
over it interrupted his progress for the moment.

There seems to us too much that is vivid and
original in this kind of play to call it imitative. It
uses and adapts experiences, rather than mimics
them solely. In fact, it may be the vehicle for childish
fantasy, as in the case of a little girl who was putting
her baby to bed. The other child's part as the baby
was to squeal loudly, whereupon the mother hurried
to her, anticipating possible demands, asking,
"What's the matter? You want water, candy?" mak-

ing all the responses that she would like her mother to make under similar circumstances.

At first the experiences recalled are those that have been most intimately felt, like the one just cited. A child's responses are made and his impressions gained through his muscles and senses. Things done to his own person and by his own body rouse the surest and deepest affective responses. Going to bed, with all its attendant skirmishes, bathing, toileting, eating, going to the doctor, being sick and taking medicine, are early and intense experiences. Dramatic rehearsal of them arouses interest and exhilaration; it stimulates an attempt at recall of details, and is the only form possible to children whose language cannot yet serve them for narration. Deriving from a common fund of experience, it has distinct social value, as all children can enter in, and each can contribute without a distinct plan of action, which, of course, would be beyond their powers. Furthermore, it progresses by steps that can be recorded, from simple to more complex, from the familiar and self-experienced to the shared and observed.

The first dramatic productions noted are hardly more than gestures. No cast is assembled; and though the materials and the activity may remind a child of a situation in which some details were similar, as in the pony incident, the properties will be few and suggestive rather than representative.

To set a table, teacups and spoons are not necessary. Two three-year-olds announced that they had ice cream. One of them placed two unit blocks on the table and called, "Audrey, bring the spoons." The other child, with no hesitation, ran to the block shelves and took two posts, units cut in halves lengthwise, and laid one at each "plate," in quite an appropriate relationship.

Though these intimate personal experiences hold their dramatic charm during all the early years of life, there soon are added recalls of events in which the child has shared, perhaps as an observer only. Driving a car, getting oil and gasoline, cooking, milking the cows, construction work, digging, painting the house, running a fire engine or being one, and even unfamiliar episodes like dining at a roof garden, often figure in play activities. Homely events, most of them are, in which the recall is almost entirely concerned with the personal aspects or the work aspects of each situation.

Through dramatic play the school hears echoes of the summer holidays or a trip at Christmas, but usually after quite an interval. Impressions seem to have to lie quiescent for a time before they bear the fruit of expression. All these things the teacher observes; and she tries to see the school and the educational process in relation to this tendency to rehearse, which runs through practically all children's play activities. That it gives them keen delight is unquestionable. That it becomes more detailed and holds the attention of more children for a longer interval when it is encouraged and when concrete materials are available for use as symbols is also certain.

What are children doing beside just remembering

past experiences? They are, by the method of re-hearsal, testing out their acquaintance with the world, establishing their orientation in some aspect of it. They are clarifying their observations, normally keen and detailed till dulled by lack of exercise and by the impatience and haste of the adult world. They are calling upon native resources of imagination and ingenuity to set their stage and work out their drama. Realism engages their attention and interest, but imagination is called upon for the reproductions they devise.

"I'm believing that this is a bus," Carl says of a packing box. Generally the make-believe is not asserted. "This is the fire engine, and you don't have to say 'red light, green light,' " Benny remonstrated to Tony, who was concerned with traffic signals. The fire engine remained motionless on the floor, and there was no pretense of arranging signals; but the drama enacted, the noise of the rushing engine and the hiss of water as it poured over non-existent flames, meant detailed and accurate observation as well as fruitful imagination.

What you see depends upon your age. At two and three an engine is noise and movement; a motor car is tires, horn, and steering wheel. At five, it can be reproduced, complete with running board, windshield, and dials, by means of blocks, boards, and kegs. The commercial toy automobile only moderately aids imitative play, for all that is left to do is to run it. As a locomotor vehicle, it serves; and its form adds to the pleasure a child has in that kind of toy.

It stimulates the recall of mental images; but there is no expression or transference of those images, as there is when the process of construction follows the memory of an experience and the impulse to rehearse it.

The impressions of two- and three-year-old children are clear; but the processes of which they are aware are the more obvious ones, and the details that they reproduce are simple. Anything that links a new experience to the personal life of a young child seems to enhance its value. That, of course, is a general axiom not limited in application to the young. It is equally true of the four- and five-year-old children; but their interests have extended, they are able to formulate questions and to see relationships where the younger ones see only discrete phenomena, and their imagination has so grown by the experiences it has fed upon that they can make the same materials tell a much more complicated story than even three-year-olds can.

If this thesis is accepted: that dramatic play is one of the keen native interests of childhood; that by means of it a child is orienting himself in a world of complex processes and intricate relationships; that it helps in the cultivation of accurate observation, imagination, and constructive ingenuity; what is the teacher's cue? Like the other impulses that her observation of children has revealed to her, she will feel that it must have room to grow to advantage: that without its being forced or exploited, the school program must direct it and give it scope and continuity.

### THE NEED FOR SELECTIVE TEACHING

Children's interests, even those most capable of constructive growth, are so evanescent and fleeting that a maturer intelligence than theirs must be at hand to make certain decisions and to redirect certain tendencies. The teacher has dared, for instance, to limit the play materials to those which she believes will aid her in encouraging good play habits. By this she means the ability to bring to play an attitude of growing interest, to set oneself to work, and to keep oneself employed at play that gives a maximum of satisfaction while, so far as she can see, it is following the course of the maturing powers.

Again, she has dared to prescribe to some extent the conditions under which play shall go on. She has found that children's block play is more profitable if their constructions are made individually, so she assigns a place for each child to build or avoids confusion by saying, "Joe is making that. There is a big space for you over here." Cooperative construction on a simple scale can be carried on with the outdoor play material by fairly mature children even in the youngest group; but until she knows the capacity of each child, the teacher encourages individual work. Indoors, where the space is more restricted, it is established as a general rule that one builds first and then, if one likes, joins other children in play with the structures. The capacity and the development of the individual can be more accurately observed and more successfully encouraged under such a program.

The teacher has also a responsibility to be the judge of the worth of activities she sees going on. She must evaluate them not only by the impulses from which they spring but also by their direction and the relevancy of their content. Gangster play, to give a concrete example, is sure to crop up in urban groups. Guns, robbery, and violence, are appealing to most children. They are a feature of the modern environment, but our teacher tends to divert and to discourage dramatic productions which deal with this phase of modern life. They are destructive rather than constructive. They lead to no further understanding of processes in the modern world, because those involved represent only disorder; or of relationships, because these concern a complex social and political situation which would be entirely beyond the realm of childish understanding even if we should regard acquaintance with it as being desirable.

The teacher finds that if the interest in construction goes along with dramatic play, the drama is carried further and has a better chance of being understood and shared by all the children concerned than if materials are not used. Therefore, if a child's imagination is working in thin air, she is very likely to make some such remark as, "You can make a bed or a stove with blocks, if you like." She will prevent a disagreement from checking good play, by a suggestion, "Here is a seat for that extra man," offering a keg which will extend the capacity of an overcrowded packing-case truck and prevent bad feeling. She may ask a question or make a suggestion which will take play a step further or make cooperation with another child profitable, if she judges that a child is repeating a plan he has used before or is showing a lag in interest: "Do the men working on your skyscraper know that Barbara has a restaurant?" or, "If the man unloading your steamer needs a truck, you could make one at the bench."

Especially does she watch the course of the play to know when an additional group experience is necessary to give the children information for which she sees they are ready or to act as a general stimulus to recreate interest. Play does go stale when a small group of children meets day after day under the same conditions. She watches for her lead or makes it. Two children have harnessed two of the small carpenter's horses and have ridden them about the playground. Now they have put pails over one end for nose bags and are waiting for the beasts to take their noonday meal. "What has your horse for his dinner, Kenneth?" the teacher asks. "Some cereal," says Kenneth. "Mine has spinach," volunteers Joe, observing nursery school precedent.

The next day comes a trip to a stable, where Jack, the stable boy, does the honors and is added to the list of friends of the fours. The children are allowed to push down some hay through the chute into the mangers and to see where the bags of oats are kept. They must be careful to close and latch the door of the feed box, for Blackie has been known to open it and eat himself sick. Animals are almost human. Jack demonstrates making the horses' beds and brushing their coats. The children ask their own questions, though the teacher occasionally interjects, "What do you suppose that is for?" or some such remark, to make sure that relevant details are observed. After this first-hand investigation and a group discussion of the trip, Kenneth and Joe may add, as a thriller, the episode of Blackie stealing oats; but they are not likely to put cereal and spinach into his nose bag.

Other subjects, not undesirable in themselves, but of such a nature that they yield no really first-hand experience, so that all that is gained by the children is information about something, an intellectual conception, seem inappropriate to these early years when thought is awakened and when it takes action in feelings, muscles, and senses.

The subject of wild animals and their ways, for example, is a debatable interest for very young children. The zoo, the collection and care of its animals, is one of the admirable provisions that large cities make for the education and entertainment of their citizens. Adults get so much diversion from visiting there that they offer it to their young early and often. Considered as one of the means of orienting young children in a world which is, after all, an unexplored field, it seems to us valueless and positively confusing. This we try to explain to parents, so that they will spend the week-ends in excursions that are more in line with the school's procedure.

Our action is similar in regard to the circus. Its reverberations in school are almost always over-stimulating, tending to lead to excitement and disintegrating play. The show, as a show, has no unity or organization from the little child's viewpoint. It is a series of unexplained unrelated happenings, and it either disturbs his interest in everyday pleasures and whets his appetite for more spectacles, or means only noise, heat, and confusion, which exhaust or frighten him. Later in his life, when his own relationships are more assured and he is more aware of himself and his place in the world, the amazing events in the circus fall into place among the romantic episodes that still come to vary the flavor of the known and thoroughly tasted.

Our teacher gives no encouragement to circus play, offers no alluring materials or suggestive remarks that would further it, and lets it exhaust itself for want of digested information that would carry it. Again she has assumed the privilege of the mature individual to make a choice as to the activities and interests to be cultivated and those to be discouraged or neglected.

The technique of trips, and their place in the program of four- and five-year-old children, will be discussed in a later section.* All I wish to do now is to add to the picture of our teacher's responsibility this further detail of administration which gives her control of a situation the main thread of which she has quite definitely in mind.

* The later section to which Miss Johnson refers was never written. However, excerpts from an earlier discussion of Miss Johnson's on the same subject appear in Part II of this book under the title of Extending the Child's Environment.

Here are these children set down in the midst of an industrial civilization which, complex and confused though it is, nevertheless, carries on the processes which have to do with the daily life of all people. We see that their play reveals a curiosity about such activities as housing, foods, transportation by land, sea and air, traffic, construction and city housekeeping, not in these adult and sober terms but as things-going-on which they see and hear, and to which they in some fashion accommodate, as they are taken about the streets by parents or friends.

Because they are children of the twentieth century, the machine and its work captivates them. Because they are going sometime to be "big workmen," the street cleaner, the window washer, the construction laborer are worth long moments of intense scrutiny; because they are social beings, acquaintance with any of the men whose work they are watching or with their animal helpers adds the warmth and pleasure of companionship to the zest of adventure.

"Mr. Marino (the grocer) said good morning to me when I came to school today."

"The policeman took us all across the dock street, when we went to see the Savannah Line steamer."

Dick, the milk horse, Fanny, the laundry horse, and Buster, the lumber horse, are distinct personalities and valued acquaintances.

Movement, sound, human activity, and social relationships—these are the external elements that attract children; and first-hand investigation into their sources seems to paint the actual world in clearer colors and to extend its boundaries.

All this discussion may serve to clarify a suspicion I voiced earlier that the teacher's own attitudes and interests color her program and techniques. Our teacher has visions of a new social order. She is convinced that however and whenever it may come, the best preparation that can be given children is, first and indispensably, to preserve and nurture their native inclination and ability to observe the phenomena within their world and to record somewhere or other, in muscle fibre or nerve tissue, the images they have gained. In addition, opportunities must be given them through which they may be equipped with an interest in situations that present problems, with the inclination to think rather than to avoid thought, with the ability to recognize relationships which exist between the events observed: opportunities which will quicken imagination so that they can see beyond the obvious, and will inoculate them with a zest for real experiences and activities so that they cannot tolerate an existence that offers nothing but vicarious adventures.

She hopes that experience in their social community, the school, will prepare children for meeting their fellows anywhere, inasmuch as relationships here are based on fair play and the techniques used have been developed in the course of living together.

« « « « « « « « « « « » » » » » » » » » » »
# PART II
« « « « « « « « « « « » » » » » » » » » » »

## Foundations for a School Philosophy

*Growth as a Basis for Curriculum*

*Adaptation as a Goal, in Contrast to Training*

## Working Hypotheses of a Nursery School

*Play Activity as a Medium of Growth*

*Extending the Child's Environment*

*Teacher, Child and Program*

*School: The First Step beyond the Home*

## EDITORIAL NOTE

THOUGH the section which follows has been composed from excerpts from Miss Johnson's writings at various times and on a variety of topics, it represents nevertheless a closely coordinated outlook on the problem of preschool education,—an outlook that is broad enough, in fact, to serve as a platform for educational experimentation at any age level. It was based, in the first place, on that principle which the modern biologist has done so much to clarify and articulate, namely the thesis that the human being is outstanding in evolutionary history primarily because his nervous system permits endless modifiability and he is consequently the most adaptable of any living organisms. The relation between such a general principle as this one and the problem of setting up an adequate environment for nursery school children is not likely to be perceived readily; it takes a rare variety of mental imagination and initiative.

It was distinctly in terms of this relation that Miss Johnson redefined the concept of habit as current in the educational world. She felt it essential to relegate the term and the idea of habit to those less important skills whose accomplishment adds only to convenience. She was intent upon distinguishing from these simple skills those more complex attitudes and tendencies which constitute the mechanisms through which the individual child carries on the "continual adjusting and readjusting" which is characteristic of him. Curriculum, program, schedule were repeatedly evaluated in terms of whether or not they really offered opportunity for independent experimentation by means of which the child could find his own way of meeting reality and gain strength in recreating it.

If the potentiality for plastic response rather than fixed response is truly an outstanding human characteristic, then surely there is no stage of human growth at which a program predominantly weighted with the learning of automatic habits is justified. In the beginning of Part II of this book, the reader will find ample illustration of the way in which Miss Johnson applied this general idea to the development of specific teaching techniques and attitudes on educational problems.

Experimental education has reduced its experience to at least one common denominator: the child must express himself. It has not as yet presented us with any final answers on the direction this expression should take at given periods of development. For the young child, one school of educational thinking believes that the child should be given maximum leeway in expressing his emotional needs though they may take the form of aggression or destruction in certain phases. In sharp contrast we find another kind of educational philosophy which is deeply convinced that children should be conditioned thoroughly and efficiently in the early years of life to social ways of behaving on the assumption that only what is learned young is learned well. Practically, the difference between these schools of educational thinking reduces itself to a difference in the ways in which they initiate children to the prohibitions of real living at the same time that they open up to them the richness of its possibilities.

It is conceded by all that maturing eventually for each individual must mean an adjustment to the reality which surrounds him. How he conceives this reality, how capable he is of affecting it, how free he is of an inner disbalance which would force him to unrealistic adjustments, depends in part at least upon his educators. The whole of Part II of this book is a digest of the daily experience of an educator in working out the equations for these none too simple problems.

The reader will probably note that many of the illustrations in the following sections are drawn from experience with the younger ages of the preschool period. This is due to the fact that excerpts from Miss Johnson's earlier writings, during a period when she was working exclusively with children ranging in age from something less than two years to over three years, have been drawn upon. In these cases the material seemed to have a significance beyond that of the particular age frequently given in illustration.

The subject matter of the following sections coincides at several points (discussions of manners, dramatic play, fundamental impulses) with that of the section on Preschool Curriculum. This has been done advisedly, since the introductory nature of the manuscript on Curriculum rendered the discussion of certain topics incomplete, and it has seemed important to us to review what Miss Johnson has written at other times, in other contexts, on these same topics.

## FOUNDATIONS
## FOR A SCHOOL PHILOSOPHY

### GROWTH AS A BASIS FOR CURRICULUM

*Each stage of growth has its own needs*

. . . We must throw away our preconceptions regarding what we like to see children doing, and we must combine what we know of biological needs with what we learn of children's interests. The balance between the two will keep us from judging an activity appropriate because children "love to do it." At two they may love to string beads, to sit long hours in a sand pile, or to listen to stories, especially if these are the opportunities which have been offered them. Since we believe that these occupations do not meet the demands of development, we shall expose the children, so far as lies within our powers, to an environment which is favorable to growth, and give them a chance to initiate their own activities. We shall observe their behavior and try to make sure that satisfaction and success attend the undertakings which are of the greatest biological service, and that more and more opportunities open up as powers develop; and we shall stand ready to make the most of further interests as they arise.

If one grants that at two, let us say, a normally developed child gets his maximum satisfaction in the free exercise of his physical powers, that his social relationships are touch-and-go affairs, and that he shows little hang-over or recall in his emotional reactions, one must recognize as a corollary that there are types of experiences that are suitable to the level attained.

We have tried to build up our procedure upon this belief regarding child development and to place our emphasis upon the importance of giving children a chance to play out the game at each level. I believe that advancing a child along one line interrupts harmony and is likely to cause a disbalance which manifests itself in emotional instability.

The physical environment contains of necessity many things which are new to a child, the use of which is hazardous. We supervise the early use of such pieces of apparatus as the slide, the seesaw, or the swings, trying to encourage experimentation but also to make sure that the first attempt will not result disastrously. Safe experimentation will lead to more experimenting and to more and more sure bodily control. Disaster tends to lead to aversion, to the development of excess caution or the setting up of fears. We try to let children learn the possibilities of the environment by exploring it rather than by taking our word for its hazards or delights. The feel in a muscle when a chair tips back, the plunge upward or downward when the weight on a seesaw is shifted, bite into awareness as words never do. Elaborate explanations defeat their own end; for though they are often not understood in a literal sense, the children use them vicariously and allow them to take the place of self-planned enterprises. . . .

*Harmonious growth means power to adjust to and exert control over the total environment*

. . . The special job that the baby has before it, is to develop an adequate physique and to learn to use it efficiently. He never puts more concentrated or more successful effort into anything than he uses during his first two years in meeting this problem, and he comes through with a more or less perfected walking technique. We wish to see the tottering, swaying, stumbling walk of the fourteen- to eighteen-month-old baby (representing an early pattern) elaborated to the ability of a sure steady control of the body in walking, running, jumping, skipping, galloping, climbing, and balancing; and further elaborated to the use of the entire musculature in combination with materials, so that the management of the body will not have to be a matter of concern but will be taken care of automatically. We wish this not only because of the physical advantage of being muscularly fit but also because of the social and psychic advantage.

There seems to be no doubt that failure to function physically on the level of the group with which one is associated stands out as one of the chief causes of maladjustment, frustration, and conflict among adults and children alike, not only because of lack of power but because of the effect of failure upon the personality. The child with a definite defect, like poor vision or hearing, a crippled hand or foot, has a very obvious handicap. I believe that a reluctance or inability to use the body freely in vigorous play with a variety of materials calls also for adjustment and tends to rouse a compensatory mechanism which is likely to interrupt the process of harmonious development. May I repeat, stating the thesis from the positive rather than the negative angle? If a child is given experiences in an environment which bids him carry on vigorous activities with the big muscles of his body, he will develop something beyond the ability to use and control his muscles. There will be less difficulty in his meeting play situations on equal terms with his mates. He can keep up with them in running, he can later meet the conditions set up by games, he can attack an adventurous situation without fear, and his body obeys the demands made by him upon it. He has not to concern himself with the effort and strain of forcing an unused or unready mechanism into new situations. Beyond this, he has an outlet for the urge to general motility, which can be said to be characteristic of the human organism. So much for the value, in development, of motor experience.

I am emphasizing the importance to the organism of the development of the larger muscles. There is not time to discuss the view which we hold, that the finer coordinations should not be stressed in the early years.

What else do these growth needs suggest? The child's incessant tendency to touch and feel, to investigate, handle, and manipulate, indicates that materials which lead to sense discrimination should be provided. Herrick, in his "Neurological Foundations of Animal Behavior," says, "Never can our thinking transcend the realm of sense experience. The most abstruse metaphysical speculation, in common with the highest flight of poetic fancy and the keenest aesthetic appreciation, is earthbound within the limits set by our physical sensory equipment." Color and weight, consistency, size, taste, and such qualities, the child comes to know and use in his play, if we plan for it in our equipment.

Growth is to what end? We seem sometimes to overvalue height and weight, and to think of growth too largely as a matter of increase in bulk. The growth we are seeking to assure for our children means their development in power and control: control of the body, a growing power to deal with the environment and to understand their relationship to it, with a resulting harmony in functioning. Our ambition for the children whose futures we are helping to shape is that they shall use to the fullest possible extent the powers given them by their physical and nervous structures, and that they shall be offered an opportunity to learn to modify the environment to their needs, on the one hand, and to adjust themselves to its conditions, on the other.

The individual comes into the world with a more or less adequate structure. He inherits, besides, a tendency to develop certain growth patterns which are more or less distinctive and individual. The conditions that have surrounded him from birth have affected for good or ill his development. Equipped with this structure, this inheritance, and this conditioning, the child enters the nursery school and proceeds to react in individual ways to the environment. We can study his equipment, the tools that are his for a lifetime, and can help to make them more effective. We can observe and modify his behavior. But between these two factors lies the force which largely determines how he shall use his equipment for living: how dynamic shall be his behavior and personality. Woodworth has called this force the "drive"; and it has to do with the life of feeling and emotion, with the affective life. We recognize it in our enthusiasms, in our affections, in our zeal, in our passions, in our ability to sustain effort; in short, in our interests. It must be conserved and protected so that the integrity and spontaneity of the affective, or emotional, life shall be maintained and shall contribute to the whole integrative process. Stability in physical and nervous structure plus stability in affective response will result in an adequately functioning human being; and that, to my mind, is the goal toward which we should strive in early education.

A third need of growth is suggested by the foregoing discussion of the affective life. A child must learn to mingle with his kind and to establish relationships with them. They are a part of his environment. As he becomes able to make these relationships successful, satisfactory to himself and his mates, he is so much further along in the integrative process.

The nursery school offers him that opportunity for social contact, and its teachers must see that the relationships that develop serve the need of his age and of the state of maturity to which he has arrived.

These then are the outstanding needs of growth which the nursery school should serve: the need for motor experiences, the need for sensory experiences, and the need for social experiences. . . .

*Observation of behavior supplies data*
*for studying growth*

. . . What is found out about physiological growth should help us in planning an environment and in our dealings as teachers with children; but probably the help it gives will be general, not particular. That is, it is interesting to know at what age the heart attains its normal size and position; how the centers of ossification form, at what ages they appear, at what rate they grow, and in what parts of the bony framework they show definite and regular age progression; but how much more suggestive these facts would be, if some inspired person could show their relationship to behavior development! I should like to see education take the lead and let these problems of habit formation, nutrition, physiological age, and so forth, be raised to illuminate the growth problems which the teacher has before her.

Let me explain my meaning. We have been making records of the behavior reactions of little children to play materials and to nursery situations in general for some years now. As we study these, we seem to find a crisis in a child's life just after he passes his second birthday. Teachers of older children tell us that in the neighborhood of seven years children pass through another epoch of change, that they want their play to take on the aspect and the seriousness of work, or at least to simulate with more exactness the work and play of older persons. The adolescent shift of interest has been recognized and studied and has its basis in well-understood biochemical and physiological changes. This twenty-fifth-month phenomenon is really startling and seems to be consistent enough to be significant.

Let us take this notion a little further. The change that we notice takes this form. Along about the twenty-fifth or twenty-sixth month we begin to note a rapid spreading out of a child's interests. His language speeds up; other performances which require fine muscle adjustments appear to become more elaborate; he makes the first of his buildings that have anything like form; and there is a further coordination of his interests. I should like to take such a fact in behavior as this and ask the anthropologist what he can find in anatomical structure or development that suggests a corresponding change. I should like a neurologist to make an attempt to trace changes in the development of the nervous system with this in mind, to see if such a sudden speeding up could be explained.

I find the specialists rather discouraging. They tell me that their measurements do not take account of the finer differences in body proportions which make you and me see one child as a little baby and another of the same age as a little boy or girl. We know that the one child suggests to us the foetus, with a big head, bulbous trunk, and small folded-up legs; and that there is maturity in the proportions of the other. You and I are pretty sure, too, that these differences in maturity of proportions are accompanied by differences in behavior, social adequacy, general attitudes, and stability. Let us find these differences and turn them back to the specialist, to see if he cannot then give us reasons.

If children go through a period of rapid growth just after two, what does this mean in school terms? What does a before-two lose or gain by being constantly associated with his superiors in understanding and performance? How much does he see of their superiority? How much do their matured activities stimulate him to reach ahead too far beyond his grasp for his best integration?

We have not time to go into the details of this twenty-fifth- and twenty-sixth-month spurt in growth, even if I were prepared to present an organized thesis upon it; but let us see what can be said about the preceding months.

The baby of two years or less presents a fairly definite picture to those of us who have been dealing with him in our families or in schools. Aside, now, from such things as his mental and physiological status, we, the laymen, expect certain things of him. We expect him to be dominated by certain interests; to be acquiring certain skills; to understand certain relationships; to respond in a fairly definite way to social stimulation; and in a sketchy way, which will rapidly become more concrete and constant, to take certain responsibilities. I will elaborate upon this formidable array of active responses a little later.

How have we built up this picture? How do we know that our standards are not too high? As far as we have been honest in challenging our opinions, we have formed them by observation of babies from walking age on. However, that is not all; for we must be raising questions and getting the children to give us the answers. That is, we must present situations to which the children will respond (or will fail to), in order to construct our age levels. We must accumulate our evidence. Then we shall have many other problems to present to our specialists. Let us go back to those great expectations of ours.

What are the dominant interests of these babies? We will set some of them in a nursery school environment and watch. I will take the setting most familiar to me. Here is a large, sunny, out-of-door space. There are raised thresholds, from roof playground to toy-shelter, and a curb bounding the pebble pit. There are large blocks stacked against a wall, large and small wagons and wheelbarrows, swings, a slide, large packing cases, planks.

Taking the sixteen- to twenty-month-old children, we find first that a study of the index preceding each week's record reveals something rather significant in the list of topics checked. They are: creeping, sitting, walking, rising; fingers, hands, mouth; curb, sill, stairs.

The pieces of out-of-door material mentioned are the slides, planks, swings, swinging rope, pebbles, sand, and wagons. Brooms, balls, and hammers, are also mentioned as being carried about. To get the real meaning of this list in age terms, we must know what the children did with these pieces of play material. The thing that we found presented to us to record was their use of their bodies. There was some creeping, still; little running; and a good deal of finding their own way over obstacles. Going on to materials used, we find slides, swings, and planks, mentioned very often, all of which involve large muscles and the same sort of exercises. Brooms, balls, and hammers, apparently are not sought for their use but as accessories to the walking problem or for manipulation. No sweeping was done with brooms, no real throwing with balls; and hammers were sucked and "flapped" (claw end, likely as not) at a block; wagons were pulled awkwardly, and no attempt was made to disengage them when they caught. Evidently, an understanding of the problems involved with such materials was beyond these children.

The kind of individual whom we all admire, and whose educational experiences we should like to reproduce, if possible, is, I believe, the one whose thinking is clear: who notices logical sequences, who sees the relationships or possible relationships between the different kinds of experiences or facts or events with which he is dealing. It is not the human encyclopedia or rapid calculator that makes us pause and admire, interesting though it may be to be able to summon dissociated facts to mind on demand, check figures before the adding machine can total them, or remember addresses and telephone numbers.

What sort of "thinking" do we expect the before-two child to be doing? The hammer, the nail, and the block into which the nail can be driven, may not represent to this child of ours a configuration which he at once completes by setting and driving the nail; but there are many relationships that he does see. He will duck his head to avoid bumping it as he goes under a table. He will hold his head up as he slides head first, so that his nose will not bump in the pebbles. He will know how to raise and tip his cup so that he can drink, and will do a rather creditable piece of work in feeding himself. He may not be able to get such spatial relationships as the place of his chair and the table where his mug of milk is; that is, he may not yet have built up the pattern of table-mug-chair-with-me-in-it so distinctly that he will automatically push the chair up into place. He will be attempting it, however. There are some figures which he has made into a pattern, especially those concerned with feeding. The dietitian-food-bib one is so well set that any one detail will suggest the others. He assumes the prescribed patterns on the slide and "lies down and turns over" at the head of the chute. He is conditioned, if you like, to this reiterated direction firmly associated with the balcony from which the slide descends.

I have not undertaken here to check up on indoor material, for what I am presenting are, after all, merely samples of a method; but in speaking of the relationships which a very little child sees, I must cite their building. Frequently blocks are sought only in order to carry them about; but when we find building there seems to be little recognition of differences in size in relation to the stability of a tower. We find children piling a series of graduated blocks like the Montessori pink tower in a sequence far from accurate and attempting to balance the largest, perhaps, on an irregular pile topped by a smaller block. We find them pressing their blocks down on a tower; and they rarely make an attempt to even edges.

I have probably used too many examples to illustrate my meaning, which is: that there are certain native interests that children show; that as far as we know, these interests are important for their favorable development; and that in the course of pursuing these interests, causes and effects become known to children, so that these relations are used in appropriate situations.

If we compare the kinds of relationship that children do get by themselves, or that they are inclined to work for, we find that they also are those which contribute to the general orientation of their bodies in the environment. They are also biologically useful. . . .

Now if we shift forward to two years, what changes do we find? As far as I can see, the development has been along two lines: first, toward the acquisition of more bodily control, and second, an extension of interest into a wider range. In other words, at two the drive toward activities that demand integrated action of the muscular system is still as strong as it was at sixteen or eighteen months, but the patterns are growing more elaborate and are being used not entirely for their own sake. Running is no longer a toddle or a trot but may be a gallop or a series of emphasized steps, and is used to get to a desired place. Jumping may be little more than a rehearsal but is used over curbs or slight elevations; and the hands, head, and arms, begin to work with legs and trunk as a harmonized whole.

A wagon may be carried in tow and hauled about corners. More kinds of material are chosen for use, and more kinds of use are made of them. Previously the experiments carried on by the children were largely with their bodies, even when the apparatus was involved. Getting into a swing or on to a kiddy kar were stunts enough. Now trying out one's powers on the kar, pedaling up a slope and coasting down, are feats beyond the powers of most twos, but stars to which they seem to have their wagons hitched. Making the swing go by oneself is another problem which is distinctly on the program at two.

Hammers, nails, and blocks, have gained the attention so that the technique of driving is well on the way. Blocks are shifted and stacked, still; that is, there is very little real construction and that only sporadic or occurring in individual cases of special maturity;

but such material as interlocking blocks and Montessori cylinders present problems that a two-year-old sees. One may say that the total configuration or Gestalt of these materials and their use has been grasped and can be dealt with, as the other one of hammer-block-nail has been.

I could go on enumerating materials and describing two-year-old use of them, but here is enough evidence to illustrate the activities. . . .

*Acquiring habits of self-help should be
a gratifying adventure*

. . . Keeping in mind that we are discussing children well under school age, what are some of the procedures for which we shall desire them to assume responsibility, and how shall we attempt to put them in the way of accepting responsibility?

First on the list I shall place the responsibility for carrying on their own play activities, for being able to choose an occupation and to work at it with a minimum of dependence upon adults or other children. This ability cannot just happen. It implies at the outset a set of responsibilities for adults which they must face very frankly. They must provide an adequate play space; they must furnish play materials which are suited to the child's stage of development; they must place these where they are accessible to the child; and they must give him enough supervision so that he will gain a degree of satisfaction from his play which will send him back to the material. At the same time they must figure so unobtrusively that the child will not get the sense that adults and adult direction are essential features of his play. Activity purposefully directed is one of the most valuable human powers, and we must learn to recognize the purposefulness of the young child's play as surely as we do that of the brick layer's work, the engineer's, or the artist's. . . .

I have put this responsibility first, not only because it seems to me the most difficult to establish and the most essential in character building, but also because, if we set it as a prime requisite in education, we are more likely to see training in routine habits in its proper perspective and relationship. I think we all agree that habits gain in importance as they become so automatic that they are no more a matter of concern; but we probably differ in regard to the time when the responsibility for them can be shifted from the adult to the child. The fact that when certain habits are thoroughly acquired we adults are also free for more congenial occupations may make us more determined in the training program we institute.

Habit training for young children is usually understood to be concerned with such processes as elimination, feeding, and self-help in dressing, undressing, and bathing. These habits are of great importance in physical and social growth, and of necessity bulk large in the program of a child from birth till they are well established. Though children seem by temperament and endowment naturally inclined to anarchy, they fortunately do appear to thrive on an orderly regime and even to enjoy it. Their apprenticeship is served during the early months when their schedule of changing, bathing, feeding, sleeping, and exercising, bounds their horizon. Cheerful acceptance is all that is asked of babies; and though some may register strenuous objection and resentment, the normally favored child succumbs with a good grace to his daily routine long before the runabout age is reached, and even in many cases goes so far as to object to a deviation from it. His acceptance is the beginning of responsibility.

How early shall we expect a child to acquire bladder control, so that he can be made responsible for his schedule? When ought he to feed himself entirely, and to take off and put on his own clothing? What standard shall we accept as satisfactory? What shall be our training procedure, how early shall we begin it, and what method of enforcement shall we use? These are questions which I shall not try to answer categorically, and which every mother who has succeeded in training her child can answer with respect to herself and her own child or children, but, of course, for no one else and no one else's child.

The important feature of this discussion, it seems to me, is first to get this question of the formation of physical habits into its proper place in education. That children must acquire these habits, there is no doubt; that a training period is necessary for their acquirement is no less true; that the individuals concerned must assume the burden of seeing that these processes are put in operation when called for, constitutes a part of growing up. But our weighting of them in the scheme of things should always take into consideration the fact that these habits are servants in the hierarchy of learned reactions and attitudes which make up the individual's stock of resources. They are not ends in themselves but means to the end of independent existence in a social world. In other words, we introduce children to certain processes not only because the activities are themselves a satisfaction but because they make a permanent addition to the resources of the individual. Banging with a hammer is fun in itself, but it also gives acquaintance and facility with a tool that holds constructive possibilities for years to come. Bouncing on a springboard apparently gives enormous immediate satisfaction to the young, and it establishes muscular control which is lasting. On the other hand, brushing teeth is brushing teeth and nothing more. Lacing shoes is, at a certain stage of the game, an absorbing occupation as well as a declaration of independence. By the time it has served the latter purpose, the child has tried all the variations in shoe lacing that can be devised by the most ingenious; his fingers have become skillful, the process has become automatic and of no further value in education, and he can turn his full attention to learning to coast down a springboard on a kiddy kar or to making a train shed for his cars.

Just there is expressed the essence of habit training and its purpose: to establish the child as an independent and self-sufficient being and to make the processes of self-help automatic so that he will be freed from attention to them and can use his resources for more creative and dynamic activities.

Pedagogy has always concerned itself with the learning process. Those of us, whether parents or teachers, who have to do with the rearing of babies should set ourselves the task of finding out how they learn and how we can most effectively use the interests that develop with growth, to establish desirable techniques. We shall find, I believe, that the chief subject of our study will be muscular exercise and control.

We have already learned one pedagogical precept which we shall do well to apply: namely, that habits are most readily formed when the process itself, or the attendant circumstances, bring satisfaction. If washing the baby's face means getting soap in his eyes, he will develop after a while a deep reluctance toward washing up. But a very persistent negativism toward being washed can be broken down entirely by a humorous approach which makes a playful game of it. This obvious example has application over a wide field.

Children differ in regard to the age at which permanent bladder control is established. I am inclined to believe that it is much more a matter of their body build or physical constitution than of their training. Otherwise, how is it that the child who has never been reproved for wet clothing or exhorted to keep himself dry, often begins to make his wants known long before one who has had months of conscientious and intensive training? Real enuresis is a serious matter; but how early must we apply that term and a corrective treatment to the involuntary evacuation of the bladder by a baby; and how early dare an adult shift the responsibility for dry garments entirely to the child himself, visiting a penalty upon him for wet ones?

In making our decision, we must ask ourselves whether we are willing to put the emphasis of our interest and approval chiefly upon the acquisition of these techniques, which, it is true, mean much in the relief of our time and attention. Our children take to themselves the standards by which we measure and the prejudices which circumscribe us. If the baby always gets our attention and applause over the exhibition of a hand activity like unbuttoning his coat, while his climbing on a table we take with alarm or else with lack of special interest, he is likely to pursue only the occupations which develop his small muscles.

My plea is not that we make no demands upon our children for the care of their bodies but that we suit our requirements to their developing abilities. It is most important that they establish in regard to food, for instance, a normal interest and anticipation, an appetite that will ensure its being taken, and an internal mechanism for assimilating it. A baby's interest in feeding himself rouses early, but the complete technique which will carry him through an entire dinner on his own power, especially after the appetite is somewhat satisfied, should not be expected of him for some years. Disciplinary measures toward the taking of food may seriously impair the normal interest in feeding. There is no rigid rule which can be guaranteed to work in every case; but we may rest assured that no healthy normal individual will continue to refuse to feed himself after he is capable of doing so with ease.

Broadly speaking, the same thing is true in regard to dressing and undressing. Here appetite does not enter in as a motive, but there is the equally impelling interest in doing for oneself. The preliminary step, it seems to me, is to develop an attention to the process in a playful way so that the baby will be aware of thrusting arms in, finding holes for toes or legs to go through, and pulling garments over the head. The next step, letting him help in the details of the process, is an easy one. The complete performance demands such continued and concentrated attention that it should not be demanded too early; and even where the interest of a child persists, indications of fatigue should be watched. It is important that the burden of having to dress himself should not outweigh the fun of accomplishment while the experience is still novel.

It is just a question of expecting from a child only as much as he is physiologically equipped to perform without undue exertion and of making sure, while the process still demands his voluntary attention, that the feeling tone aroused is one of satisfaction. He should get from it a sense of his own adequacy rather than a feeling of being approved by an adult. I believe that children will develop more reliable and more lasting facility in self-help by a process of education worked out on these lines than by intensive training and rigid demands for a consistently adequate performance. I believe, too, that this educative process will result in no loss of time, and that it will effect an appreciable spiritual gain on the part of adults and children.

*What is a realistic balance between manners*
*as a habit and genuine feeling?*

I wonder if we all mean the same thing by courtesy, or manners. If we can turn our thinking inside out and see just what it means to us, perhaps we can define it more clearly.

To me, I think, "manners" signifies the accepted techniques, or ways of doing things, that are concerned especially with social intercourse. There is a way of behaving when we meet our fellows; there is an accepted method of using one's table implements, of responding to an invitation, or of accepting a gift, just as there is a form that one must follow when presented at court.

To be unacquainted with these forms places a person at a disadvantage, unless he is too immature or too unlearned to be aware of his deficiencies. To be acquainted with them sets him at ease and allows him to be fully concerned with the more engrossing details of social relationships.

Manners are lubricators, are they not? We do not depend upon them when we have questions of efficiency or of inspiration to consider. We cannot imagine saying, "This man, an expert engineer, cannot build our bridges because he does not stand when a woman enters the room," or refusing to buy the picture of a marvelous artist because he is socially gauche. It is true that we may feel that certain useful or pleasant or fruitful avenues which might be open to these two men are closed or that they will miss certain interesting opportunities because of their social inadequacies. That, however, must be a matter of opinion; and all I am trying to do is to find out whether or not manners are a fundamental in character. At this moment I vote no on this issue and raise the point for further discussion as to whether manners can be called fundamental in social intercourse as well.

Now we come to courtesy. The Century Dictionary, after defining it as "civility, courtliness in manners, etc." adds, "especially politeness springing from kindliness of heart," which, I think, expresses what we should mean in the use of the word.

At once we realize that we are out of the realm of manners and are discussing a fundamental emotion. We appreciate the difference in our reactions to the external manner and to the inward intention. If a person hurls herself against you in a subway jam, says, "I'm sorry," and goes hurtling on her way, your sense of indignity and resentment is strong. If, on the other hand, she pauses to say, "I *am* sorry. Did I hurt you?" you react quite differently. Your adrenals are hardly called upon. You smile and assure her that it is quite all right, and, moreover, you carry no malice with you. It is conceivable, of course, that the first person was entirely well-intentioned, but lacked the capacity of identifying herself with another individual or had not the social ease which would have allowed her to express the feeling.

If we could rear children by means of a wishing ring, I think we should rub it very hard and wish for them the two traits expressed in that sentence: a real feeling about the things that affect the persons with whom they come in contact, and the God-given ability of expressing that feeling with freedom and grace.

In the process of defining courtesy, we have also defined the concept of consideration, have we not? Consideration certainly implies an identifying of oneself with another person so that the same sort of interest and effort is called into play in dealing with him as one would employ in one's own behalf. Stated thus, it seems a pretty exalted point of view and probably is an exaggeration of the best we desire for our children. The impulse to serve oneself first, most, and oftenest, dies only in the especially sanctified and is so closely tied up with the impulse of self-preservation that we should not, and certainly do not, expect or desire quite this degree of self-immolation. As I said before, we wish genuine feeling and the ability to express it.

What are our aims, then, for our children?

As far as I am concerned, I can say that I should wish a child to have a friendly attitude toward his mates and toward strangers, both adults and children; to be responsive to things, people, and events, which affect them, their composure, their pleasure, and their pain. Second, I should wish him to be able to communicate this attitude by some technique, conventional or otherwise. And third, I should wish him to have at his disposal the manners that are current, or perhaps I should say—considering the day and age —the manners that are most gracious and disarming, so that he can spend a minimum of thought and effort upon their details. On the other hand, I should not wish him to be so responsive to others that his whole emotional energy spent itself in that way.

How are we to make sure that even the desired externals are a part of our children's equipment?

I still believe that insistence upon conventional forms is not wise with very young children. Greetings and partings are easily disposed of but should not be required. As with discipline at meal time, insistence may develop the very attitude you are intending to avoid. "Good morning" and "goodby" should be spoken gaily, not unwillingly or as a duty. "Please" and "thank you" should be said for the child on appropriate occasions, to accustom him to the habit; then he may be reminded to say them, but not disciplined, till he does.

For the rest, he should not be allowed to treat people ruthlessly; but I think an appeal to him to show generosity or sympathy or grief is not only vain but positively debauching: debauching, because it cultivates the expression of a feeling that does not exist.

Neurologists are telling us that training in certain types of behavior is quite useless until the suitable neurological connections have been established in the brain. Sometime the biochemists are going to be able to give us an exact measure for the state of maturity of the emotions. At present we can only watch and guess.

To go back: there are things that just aren't done— grabbing toys, slapping grandmothers, biting, and such barbarities; and in our school we put these prohibitions on the score of something we call friendliness. Friendly children do not knock others down or scratch grown-ups. It is not always quite so simple as that, for insistent negativism or rebelling may indicate some emotional blocking which needs investigation and treatment. We cannot stop to discuss mental hygiene here.

When can we begin a more positive training than this? At six, certainly (even, I suspect, at five), children can be interested in manners as ways that are used in getting on with people. Learning and trying out these ways should be fun not a chore. After a quarrel a discussion of the steps leading to the disagreement can be traced, and the children will be quick to recognize that a few soft words would have changed the atmosphere.

The analogy between politeness and a lubricating medium can be used in a sort of allegory or fable. Here is the wagon which was mended so that it was sound, but still groaned and squeaked so that it was a nuisance. The people who owned it could get their work done, but the noise from it was annoying and kept them from hearing each other's songs or pleasant conversation. When it was oiled, it ran without noise or friction. That is about on the level of a five- or six-year-old's imagination, and he would rather be asked to use a little oil when he says, "Give me that hammer!" or crowds in between two children talking together than he would to be called to task for being impolite.

I used to say hopefully that if one were scrupulous in politeness to children, they would acquire that habit as they do mother's peculiarities of gait and father's pet expletive. It is not so easy as that; and I wonder if the reason may not be that manners are not really a part of us as idiosyncrasies of voice, appearance, or behavior, are.

There are many reasons for the difficulties we find in establishing the habit of being mannerly and considerate. One is the obliviousness of the young to any interests but their own. Our babies, eighteen months to three years old, vary a great deal in their social responses. They acquire the habit of greetings and farewells early; and let us stop to note that these measures are rarely put on the basis of "musts" but are much more play than duty. "Please" and "thank you" are taken up fairly readily in our circles, though they are not remembered invariably and always seem to evaporate in an emergency. They are given along with the technique for getting from another child a desired toy. "If you ask him, I think he will let you have some."

We find our present group very mature and casual in their conversation. They often say "Hello" much as we do, meaning "Oh, there you are," and they bid farewell to parting guests or friends as a matter of course. On the other hand, they were strikingly immature about sharing toys when they returned after the summer, having attained the advanced age of two and a half. Not only would they descend upon a child who had chosen a wheelbarrow or a doll and covers, and would, with set jaws and gleaming eyes, seize her toys like bandits; but when this attack failed or was thwarted, they would demand of an adult with utter assurance "I want that," apparently of a mind that might makes right.

After four weeks of these strong-arm tactics, it seems to have seeped through to them that such methods are not popular with grown-ups. The other day after I had told Mary that she must not seize Theresa's broom while she was still using it, but that if she waited, Theresa—who is a very little baby— would drop it, Mary was heard directing her, "Drop your broom for me. Drop it right there!" There does seem to be some confusion of thought here, and one doubts the effectiveness of an appeal to the better feelings of these savages.

This also illustrates some immaturity of feeling, does it not? Do we know how late the development of the emotional life may be delayed? Read the

"Innocent Voyage," by Richard Hughes and you have a very sensitive narrative of the emotional reactions of still older children to a set of circumstances, some of them fantastic, it is true, but illustrating in an authentic and consistent way the utter confusion of issues and values in a child's mind.

I have been trying to suggest in these excursions into the bypaths of anecdote that the feeling which is the foundation of true courtesy does not come with early dentition. Perhaps it does begin with the permanent teeth. Justice, fair play of the sort that is applied in the nursery school, is accepted. Its rules seem within the understanding of a child, so that he can accept and apply it after a thorough introduction to it. An embryonic "friendliness" of a live-and-let-live variety seems to be practically possible if it is applied to *me* as impartially as to *thee*.

There is an ugly trait that we do not find in children, probably because of this same emotional obtuseness, and that is, holding a grudge against the wrongdoer. The only children whom I have observed showing animus of any kind have been those who have been taught that manner by long experience with older playmates who have threatened and teased.

When does "kindliness of heart" arise as a real honest-to-goodness feeling? Perhaps you have learned from watching your groups over a long period. I can frankly say that I do not know.

Another difficulty weighs heavily on my mind. It

is the need of reiterated correction in order to get habits established. As a parent one may well resent being a thorn in the flesh. If a parent corrects enough he will be identified with correction. We have two large duties. One is to bring up our children: to teach them to do things for themselves, to make being honest and direct more enduring than being devious, to cultivate in them good taste and good manners and all the do's and don't's necessary to character development and community living; the second, to live with them in such a way that we shall be allowed to share their interests, their pleasures, their fun and foolishness, and even their escapades. The first of these jobs is distinctly the parental one and is heavily adult. The second, it seems to me, is all that makes being a parent any fun at all.

My only recommendation about the manners end of this job is that we give these reminders as inconspicuously as is consistent with clarity and that we never interrupt vital concerns to obtrude them. Your child gets an inspiration for a poem, then gives it to you to read while his eyes are still glowing with the joy of creation. Is this, I ask you, the moment to correct his spelling? Yet I assure you it has been done. He comes home full of the excitement of a football match, does not take his hat off as he pulls the score out of his pocket, does not see that his grandmother has come to tea, and does not apologize when he steps on his mother's toes. Must a parent check all his enthusiasm in the cause of civility or may she take this tide at its flood, call upon grand-mother to share the fun, and take up the question of correct deportment at a later time? The relationship between child and parent needs to be safeguarded. You would not wish to lose out on the man-to-man attitude that your child may hold toward you for twice the stock of manners he may have in his possession.

Have you any lead on this subject? When, under what circumstances, do children most easily forget their manners? Is it when they are under the influence of some strong interest? Are not adults very similar to them, as a matter of fact, in this? What sort of child is most susceptible to manners? I have a con-viction that some are born with a natural immunity and that they will get attacks later than the sus-ceptible subjects. Can it be that the children who are most independent, whose activities are important to them, whose interests are keen and easily aroused, are later in picking up conventions than the less dynamic and creative children?

As to the responsiveness that makes us considerate of other people, can we do more than illustrate it? If we are even approximately what we wish our chil-dren to be, that is, if we are truly generous and honest and fearless, and if we are living on such a plane with them that our relationship is genuine, I believe these attitudes become a part of our children's characters.

This youngest generation is tremendously inter-esting to me. I find them amazingly mature in their judgments and in their emotional expressions (and now I am including more than courtesy) but extraordinarily simple and direct in their relationship to each other. Some of our considerateness is sentimentality. That makes no appeal to these clear-eyed young persons. Some of our generosity is given in a niggardly spirit. We are generous to be generous. They share as a matter of course, expecting no credit for it. They cry less over spilt milk than any children it has been my luck to know, and perhaps this is the reason they sometimes appear hard. They do not grieve over a past disappointment, and they are impatient of whimperers. They are not like my generation. They are no more like yours. Probably they are not quite like any other. But though I cannot say that I thoroughly understand them, and though they frequently rouse my ire, especially when my emotions are not entirely within control, I think they are far and away the most interesting and important product this old world has ever found upon itself. Long life to them, and if we don't like their manners, we can realize that they don't like ours any better.

*Is thumb-sucking a bad habit or a faulty adaptation?*

May I say in introduction that we have tried in planning our school organization to study children and to find out through what kinds of activities and experiences that can be called biologically useful they seem to get satisfaction. By and large, these appear to be activities with their bodies and senses; experimentation in new fields with materials and with other children; and rehearsal of their experiences through some media or by some means that give them emotional release and raise their general affective tone. Consequently our task has been to provide the equipment which would make such a program of activities possible.

In general we have tried to approach the question of undesirable habits from a very untechnical but, it seems to me, logical point of view. The child under discussion comes to us from a situation (the home, in this instance) in which he has built up certain unfortunate responses. He comes into a new environment which is, in and of itself, an interruption to the processes going on, good as well as bad. This proves itself over and over. A baby came to us with a vocabulary including thirteen words no one of which we heard at school for at least a month after entrance. Similarly, children frequently break down all their habits of bladder control for a period after entering the nursery school. That the opposite is also true, I hardly need to say. The question we ask ourselves is, can we establish a new set of interests and give an opportunity for these interests to function so satisfactorily that there will be an increase in mental health?

Our practical procedure in the matter of thumbsucking is this: it is an infantile habit which by the time babies come to us has served its end, if end it had. On the other hand, it distinctly gives the child satisfaction of a sort through a means that is of no biological use and does prevent his setting up other more mature responses to his environment which will serve his growth. There are standards of maturity at every age level; and if a child has to get his satisfaction from responses distinctly below his own expected maturity, we regard it as a problem. At a certain stage, for example, probably before two years, a child confronted with a basketful of his clothing will be likely, while he is being dressed, to pick out the various articles and throw them to the floor. This is his idea of a good joke. It should be replaced soon after two years by another set of interests, usually the selection of appropriate articles and the attempt to share in the dressing process. In general, we may say that any normally living human being gets more satisfaction from maturity than from immaturity. It is one of the most acute psychological problems which we have to face, not only as children but also as adults.

Our attack upon thumb-sucking in the nursery school is indirect, as it is upon fears, reluctances, personal preferences, dislike of the unfamiliar, and other manifestations which seem to be interfering with the individual's growth. We can succeed only by setting up a counter-program which gives an equal degree of satisfaction.

Thumb-sucking is likely to be especially persistent at nap time. As a routine, we put our children into sleeping bags, unless there is something against it. The reason for this is chiefly that, thus, they will remain in bed and covered, and can be left without close adult supervision. This procedure automatically interrupts the habit and in the majority of cases is an effective measure. Occasionally, however, the deprivation tends to increase the desire and interrupt the nap. In these cases we make it possible for the baby to find his thumb and indulge himself rather than to allow a resistance to naps to persist. All the way along, however, we attempt to take advantage of the increasing feeling of familiarity and security which the nursery school builds up in children and to press this mechanical interference to sucking as far as we can without disturbing the child. It is unnecessary to say that we try never to let the child know that we are interested in his habit and *never* put any undesirable habit, or a desirable one, for that matter, on a moral plane.

Thumb-sucking, however, is not confined to nap time. As I have watched our thumb-suckers, it has seemed to me that it served them quite distinctly as a retreat, as a way to avoid or to compensate for an unwelcome situation. They suck when kept from other activities, as when put on the toilet. Our method is to give small objects which attract and which take two hands to manipulate. They suck when bored or fatigued. We set up a compelling occupation or give a diversion that will rest at the same time that it absorbs a child. They suck when thwarted. We make sure that the child's effort comes through to a conclusion satisfactory to him or that an acceptable substitute is offered. The wheels of his cart lock with those of another. He may give up supinely and retire to his ever ready solace, his thumb. We plan never to let his effort end in that kind of failure, but to give him enough help and encouragement to make sure that the activity does not subside incomplete and unfulfilled. Furthermore, we scrutinize with the parent the home and school procedure, to make sure that there are no extreme standards being set up. This, I am sure, is valid for all sorts of undesirable habits: enuresis, nail biting, and stuttering, as well as thumb-sucking. No surer road to such inappropriate and unproductive patterns as these can be found than the setting up of standards beyond the child's ability to attain or foreign to his interests.

The cases in which thumb-sucking has persisted in the face of a truly unemotional attitude about it on the part of adults, and in a program which gives a child the fullest opportunity to follow his own interests, have seemed to me to be due to some inadequacy in the biological mechanisms: a physical deficiency or a serious lack in emotional satisfaction, or both. In the cases of two children who come to my mind at once of whom this was true, each had a younger brother or sister before he was two years old; and in both cases the advent of the baby had been attended by a rather serious interruption in the routine of the child under discussion. In both cases, too, there were certain physical handicaps which interfered with normal development.

# WORKING HYPOTHESES OF A
# NURSERY SCHOOL

## PLAY ACTIVITY AS A MEDIUM OF GROWTH

. . . The nursery school must build up desirable play habits. It can do this only if it regards the play activities of children as important assets in education, and if educators have a philosophic as well as a practical attitude toward the educational process and are willing to say what kinds of persons they hope to find in the world as a result of modern schooling.

The nursery school, studying the behavior of young children, must offer them materials, equipment, and set-up, which will serve certain universal impulses equally characteristic of all ages. These may be stated in various ways, but I should like to discuss them in terms of the children's observed responses: the activity impulse, the urge toward motor and sensory experimentation; the constructive impulse, the urge to gain power over the physical environment; the ego impulse, the urge to gain power over the social environment; and the dramatic impulse, the urge to rehearse and reproduce past experiences in dramatic form.

I should then make the statement of the preschool's duties more specific than that it must provide "good toys." What sorts of play materials will give these impulses scope at different age levels? What kinds will help their growth? If these impulses remain immature or if they become misdirected, the integra-

tive process of personality development will be interrupted. . . .

*Children need to explore and*
*experiment, to create and understand*

. . . Our first responsibility is to find out what these
child organisms do in the environment that is provided for them.

After they have fairly emerged from what may
be termed the larva stage, so that they can make their
way about, we see them experimenting with their
bodies and exploring their surroundings. Babies handle; they taste, they feel with hands and mouths,
they look, and they listen; they creep and walk and
climb; later they stride, trot, jump, utilizing everything they can find in their play purpose of activity.
As we watch, we find many repetitive processes
going on, sometimes almost like practice, as when
the child takes all the blocks out of one box and puts
them into another. The more we observe, the more
we are convinced that the play of the very young
organisms of this human species we are studying is
characterized by general activity, by repetition of
the same patterns, and by general exploring reactions
directed toward the physical environment. We come
to realize also that this physical environment must
be assumed to include other individuals of the same
species, whom the child investigates much as he does
inanimate objects but whose activities are in themselves a strong stimulus to action on his own part.

At first we are inclined to consider that the primitive activities of childhood are purposeless. These small creatures deal very little at first with the playthings provided, and their span of attention is short. Then, as time goes on, we observe that our "subjects" have gradually acquired a remarkable degree of control of their own bodies and of precision in using their hands; that certain habits of busy-ness and self-dependence seem to have been established; and that there is unmistakable evidence of what can surely be called mental activity. So we conclude that the play has been biologically important. Furthermore, if we have made our observations with minds open to all impressions, we have seen evidence of a high degree of satisfaction, of elation, of joy in this early kind of play. . . . We are justly disturbed if we see a child choosing to be inactive, sedentary, silent.

There are not many years when we can depend upon the motor impulse to operate as incessantly as it does in early childhood, and it is a truism that by means of it children gain all their ordinary techniques. Walking and talking are outstanding examples. There is another quality which play exhibits: namely, the tendency to seek variety, to experiment. It sends a child in the first place to a testing out of his own powers and then to an experimental attack upon his entire environment.

These two essential characteristics of the play impulse, the tendency to be active and the tendency to be experimental, can be assets of education. They are assets, however, only if they are used. We have all seen children who were incessantly active and who had the investigating qualities of magpies, who yet showed a lack of integration in their motor impulses and a distinct paucity in their play interests. Play, no less than work, needs a shop and raw materials. The nursery school attempts to supply them in its play space and its equipment.

There are three factors to be remembered in planning nursery school education: educational objectives, the recognition of natural interests, and the environment which can serve the two ends. We as teachers are hoping to have a hand in the process of development. We shall affect it, whether we will or no. We must decide where we wish to place our emphasis, what behavior patterns and what interests we are going to nurture.

Interests will spontaneously develop out of the play impulses, given material to feed upon and stretches of uninterrupted time in which to pursue them. Our program must assure time to the children. Our equipment must meet play needs.

Suppose we give the following formulation of our educational aims. We believe that education should bring to children a gradually growing understanding of the world they live in, extending as far as their own work, their own needs, and their own experiences have led them. In other words, it should give them an alert and sharpened sense of the relationships between the factors that living in the world has brought into focus for them; and in gaining such an understanding, the children must be, themselves, active agents and participators, not disciples. . . .

We have implied that life in the nursery school should be an actively sharing and experiencing one. Children will tend to reproduce, to rehearse and elaborate their experiences in their play. It is one of their methods of organizing their observations about men and things, and of reinforcing and vivifying their past experiences. They will adapt materials as they find them, but we should make definite provision for this type of dramatizing. Children will do it with no material at all; but if they are working with "properties" like boxes and boards and blocks, or dolls and wagons and clothes, their imagination will tend to add to the scheme and depart from the first simplified attempt.

Furthermore, there is an impulse to devise, to create, which must be met. At first almost any things which can be moved about will answer. Blocks are especially well adapted to satisfy the early patterning impulse. Later, tools and wood can serve some children; clay and paints meet the needs of others. The essential thing to remember here is that in these processes the child is an artist, not a mechanic. The stirring experience comes to the child through the process of doing, not through the product which may be the tangible result.

The nursery school brings to the children a very vital social experience: that of meeting each other, sharing toys, adapting to varying personalities, and carrying on activities in which there is an increasing demand for cooperative effort. The chief concern of the school should be to make sure that the social demands which the situation makes on the children are scaled to the appropriate age level; that the age range is kept fairly narrow or the amount of space made large enough so that close-knit group play is not forced upon the children and so that social exploitation of the immature by the older is not possible.

The social impulse is universal. The power adequately to take one's place in the social group matures slowly. Because its roots are laid so deeply in the affective life, it is less safe to allow it to shift for itself than it is to allow the impulse toward physical activity to take its own course. . . .

*Play materials serve as tools for expression*

The equipment which will serve these impulses need not be invariably the same and should vary with the location of the school. From impulses such as these an urban situation will develop interests which will of necessity differ from those stimulated by the country or the suburbs. The country environment makes possible certain full body activities for which definite apparatus must be provided in the city. In the large city, roofs provide far better out-of-door space than yards, because of the sun and freedom from damp. In the country it is possible to have ground enough so that gardens can be set aside without depriving children of running space. Plants can be grown, and certain animals can be given liberty enough so that their lives will not have the abnormal restrictions of captivity. In the country the processes which the children can observe are in simpler form than in the city. The intermediary step back from the food a child eats, the house in which he lives, and the animals he sees about him, to the source of the raw materials is shorter and easier for him to follow and understand. However, if the city is his environment, the problem of presenting it to him must be met when he is old enough to add acquaintance with a larger environment to that of the school, if we accept the definitions of educational objectives given on a preceding page.

The nursery school leaders who have blazed a trail have worked out their equipment gradually as they have seen needs arising in children's play. There have been sample lists published, which probably contain far more material than any one school needs in the beginning. Very small children, perhaps, need more kinds of things than older ones, for they gain a certain maturity in perception by a superficial acquaintance with a variety of shapes, weights, textures, colors, and behaviors. The universally essential materials are those that serve the constructive interests. . . .

The child is a craftsman. Blocks seem to us the most effective and basic tools. For indoor use they must have a unit form such as the brick, and all the other varieties must be derived from this unit, multiples of it up to the quadruple or divisions of it into half units, triangles and pillars. The addition of arches and curves, of cylinders of the unit length and of two diameters, enrich the possibility of this material, especially for older children. Blocks of this sort are on the market; but unless one has seen the complexity of structures put up by young builders, the advantage of such building material over odd shapes or varieties of the cube may not be apparent. Out-of-doors large hollow blocks of two sizes, with some additional material which will be described later, lend themselves to large constructions in which, quite literally, groups can play together.

The child is an artist. Nowhere can he find better plastic material than blocks for these years when his ability to express his feelings through the medium of color or clay is limited by an immature technique. Doubtless he does not plan his structures. The startling beauty of his designs is probably the result of an inner rhythm and balance which operates through his muscles; but none the less, the satisfaction he gets is distinctly that of the creator.

The child is an actor. All situations may be dramatic to him. No episode is too slight to yield him a plot. Washing hair admits of more histrionic detail than anyone who has not seen it staged can believe. No experience is too complicated and elaborate for the child to reproduce; and again blocks give him an adequate medium, a framework for his dramatic idea. The tug steering a big liner into a dock, the dredge deepening a harbor channel, pique his dramatic ingenuity, and he has no hesitation in setting his stage for an elaborate performance with realistic detail.

In all of these activities a child uses the blocks as raw material. As his skill and understanding mature through experience, he will look about for additions to this basic tool. Colored cubes or other odd-shaped objects he will add as decoration. He will use hammer and nails to fasten bits of wood together for a railway signal, a derrick, or some other detail which his structure needs. Trains, boats, or cars, will stimulate his impulse to use blocks and to play with his construction. These accessories need not be elaborate; his imagination will take care of the details. For the most part it is motion, action, that he desires; and that his own muscles will furnish. Size is important, for the toys must be related roughly to the blocks so that they can be combined with them. The simplest sort of interlocking train is satisfactory for the first three years. After children have lived in an environment where inventiveness is encouraged, those of four and five years will add the detail that their play demands, and the six-year-old children will make toys that they need. There are, however, very well-made wooden trains of proper size on the market, if children seem to need the stimulus of different kinds of cars. A block in which the characteristic form of a truck or a taxi is roughly indicated in its shape and color meets all requirements until a child is old enough to try out his skill in the workshop. If there are older children in the school or the home, they can make these simple toys for the younger ones.

Dolls and domestic animals remain fruitful sources of interest and value in block play almost indefinitely, after they once recall to a child a real situation. At first it is difficult for him to use any substitute for himself in his drama. Later the transfer of personality is successfully made, and the *dramatis personae* can be extended to the limits of the supply of toy men and children, pigs and cows.

Out-of-doors a child will not need the same kind of accessories, since his structures made of the hollow blocks will house himself and his mates. Big packing boxes, and boards of three-quarter-inch wood about five inches wide by four or five feet long, pails, ropes, kegs, brooms, and shovels, hold a wide range of dramatic possibilities and add to the vigorous muscle-satisfying play which the apparatus is designed to serve.

We have not exhausted the subject of playthings when we center our interest about block building. Children are different and individual, different because of age, and temperament as well. When they are in the stage of exploring their environment, things to manipulate, objects which offer variety in size, form, weight, and texture, will give them valuable sensory experiences. Instruments with which they can make sounds, pleasing or cadenced, if possible—bells or a Chinese gong, for example—hold interest over a short time only, but are distinctly profitable. Balls and soft bags for throwing, discs for rolling, swings, trapezes, and rope nooses for swinging experiments, add to pleasure and to control of the body at the same time. I have spoken of wagons and kiddy kars as popular among the very young. They are, of course, also useful in dramatic play.

At the age when the dramatic imagination is centered upon experiences observed and shared in the family, larger dolls with pieces of cloth to use as clothing or bedding, flatirons, beds, and other domestic articles, should be included. Even here the rule of giving preference whenever possible to material that can be adapted to a variety of uses is a safe one. The more elaborate the details, the less opportunity is left to children for inventiveness and imagination; and in the choice of toys, the danger of overcrowding the environment with materials that suggest a rather limited use should always be considered.

There is a certain economy in a unified plan for equipment. The materials hold increasing possibilities as the children mature. Take such a thing as the interlocking train. At first the interlocking device is the interesting feature. It could be supplied by means of a "puzzle toy," something that had no other purpose than to be linked and unlinked. But after this device is thoroughly understood, the child will himself invent other play possibilities with the train, and his interest in the material is thus renewed. Material which can be used in only one indicated way is more suitable for testing purposes than for play. It makes no provision for inventiveness nor for progress in use with increasing maturity. . . .

*Dramatic play is the child's way
of organizing experience*

. . . No one who has watched children's dramatic play can doubt that it represents an authentic interest. I say authentic because, while adults tend to base their judgments of children's interests upon memories of their own and almost invariably date their appearance too early in the play life, this particular interest, its first appearance, and its early growth history, have been discovered by watching children at play. Furthermore, it is indubitably one of the methods of learning practiced by children: first to experience fully, then to recall and relive, and finally to embroider.

If education is to use as a positive asset this impulse to rehearse past events, it must be prepared gradually to extend the range of children's experiences, along intentional and related lines. It is a pedagogical truism that learning proceeds from the known to the unknown. In the education of young children the adventure into new fields must be not only *from* the familiar but *with* it as an accompaniment and a steering wheel. The jogging shuttle is a more appropriate symbol to illustrate excursions of youthful adventurers than even as slow-moving a vehicle as the ox team. Forward and back again it goes, till the new and the old are closely knit.

An event does not take dramatic form so long as it remains detached from the intimate and the personal; but sometimes in the process of making it his own, a child calls upon fantasy rather than fact. Children seek for relationships between the events which are happening about them, but their conclusions are of necessity limited by the background upon which they draw, and adults often fail them by being so diverted by childish reasoning that they do not see its promise. A fire extinguisher on a wall is called a statue because of the child's acquaintance with a figure in a niche in a familiar apartment house. If rubbers are put on, it must be raining, though there are no clouds in the sky. The moon, visible in the day time, is asserted to be the sun, and this opinion is upheld with vehemence among the very young. The city child's horse is put to bed with a pillow under its head, and the farmer in the toy village goes to the chain store for milk and takes it back to the cows.

It is part of education to make a selection from the mass of natural interests of children in the world about them and to give them the opportunity for an introduction to these various phenomena, for investigating them, for raising questions about them, and for coming into actual contact with them through play. The lines of investigation, the total mass of impressions gained by the children, the relationships which are stressed, and appropriate media for dramatic expression, remain largely in the hands of the teacher; her task is the delicate one of stimulating interest during the direct experience and of helping in the recall by shared discussion of it afterward.

The dramatic play which follows an excursion afield gives one the feeling of watching a creative process in which there is a high degree of mental stimulation and an enormous release of emotional power. . . .

. . . Dramatic play carried on without a setting in

concrete materials has two kinds of limitation. The imagination it calls upon may be dealing with fact; but since this is largely implicit, it remains with the individual originating it. It cannot to the same extent be shared and become a social undertaking. Young children depend largely upon gesture and demonstration for the communication of their ideas, even after they have acquired language facility. I believe that there is more likely to be real cooperative sharing in a group if the dramatic representations deal with actual material. Granted that this point of view is accepted, it affects environment planning. . . .

. . . It is observed that many of the activities carried on by children simulate real life situations and procedures to which the children have themselves been subjected. As the wagons are pulled, train sounds are made, and passengers are taken aboard; block piles are given names and serve as representations of houses, boats, garages, stoves, and beds. In short, we soon realize that the play materials we place in the environment have become tools with which the children can reconstruct past experiences, "properties" which serve them to make more real the scenes which they are reënacting. A shelf, an overturned table, or a line of blocks appear as a bed; and the performances familiar to mothers at bedtime take place. "I want a drink," "Please leave the door open," or long histrionic wails, are reproduced with a realism that is actually convincing. Pails are carried as suitcases; passengers climb aboard the train, which goes choo-chooing on its way. The man with candy passes through the car, and a porter helps with the luggage at the end of the journey.

With an increase of maturity in observation and in powers of mimicry, more ambitious drama is attempted; but through it all certain dominant features are common. First, actual first-hand experiences are taken as dramatic material. Early efforts have to do with the homely matters of intimate personal life; then come the events which have brought the individual in contact with the world outside his home. Second, the dramatic representation involves the use of the impulses noted in the immature reactions, the motor and sensory activities which are now directed to the end of living over and intensifying the recall of the past. Even the passengers in a block-built train are likely to make train sounds instead of keeping to their places and merely imagining the engine's progress. The child becomes the horse he is remembering and paws and neighs and tosses his head, even though his role is that of the rider. Third, through it all runs and develops the social interest, the pleasure in shared activities and play schemes, with a language accompaniment which serves as a communicating medium and also as another vehicle for dramatic pleasure.

We find, then, that the early child-play we have observed is actually useful in development, and that it keeps at high level the feeling of well-being and of joy which we believe ought to characterize childhood.

*Play schemes are a vehicle for*
*constructive social relations*

The social situation is an inherent part of the environment and a constant stimulus to the children, but no effort is made by the adults in the nursery school to lead them into it.

From the first even the very little babies watch, which would seem to indicate a certain degree of awareness. However, one begins to question how thoroughgoing that awareness is, how far it extends and can be called awareness-of-another-person-like-me, when one finds a child using another for support, pawing over him, or putting his mouth against him with an unsmiling intentness which suggests his attitude toward inanimate materials; taking toys from him or allowing the other child to take his without a flicker or change in facial expression to indicate feeling. This attitude does not last long, but there are long periods of entirely independent play when other children and their concerns do not engage attention. There is actual withdrawal from contact during play on apparatus which requires concentrated muscular balance, like the slide and planks. The high spots in social life at this age are what we call group play, when sometimes all the children choose the same or similar material or carry on similar activities at the same time. Digging in sand or pebbles, running about the playground with or without wagons, using dolls and covers, are instances. . . .

As these babies approach their second birthdays, there is less shift in their social relationships than one might expect. Susan is less inclined to use Tom as a prop when she climbs; and if she does, Tom is more aware of it and more inclined to object. There is an increasing awareness of other children and some attempts at contacts. These are, in general, of three kinds. One is to trail older children and attempt to join them: for instance, to bring up blocks and add them to an older child's building. These efforts are short-lived and ineffective. If not positively repulsed, the youthful contribution is usually ignored. A second method is to join the group in active play in which all the members are independent, as in running, riding, or sliding. A third way is by slapping or embracing, or by repulsing such approaches from others. Perhaps watching ought to be added as a social response. It holds a large place in the time distribution of a little child's day. We suspect that a sort of implicit rehearsal may be going on.

I do not mean that there are never, in our records, instances of dramatic play which included a group, or that there is never the interchange of understanding at two; but the instances are so rare that they hardly appear. There is a more mature relationship between the child and an adult than between children, and the former is usually adult-initiated. The nearest approach to social play is in the nature of looking peek-a-boo through a window or around a door at another child, laughing, retreating, and repeating. Antiphonal chanting or shouting occurs, but it is not persistent. Conversation between children is practically nil. "Mine, mine" and "No" comprehend fairly well the conversation between two's, though remarks addressed to adults often take a more mature form. . . .

. . . One of the chief reasons for the popularity of the nursery school is that it gives children the opportunity for association with others of equal age. This social experience can be gained only by means of an organized group, for the casual meetings of children in the park are not constructive even when they are not disastrous. We seem to have found that the social impulse is strong in children, that it awakens early in life, and that it is capable of a development along with that of language; so that three- and four-year-old children are carrying on social relationships which, though not close-knit, have actuality and purpose.

The reason that these relationships are successful is that the social situation is not forced upon children and there is leeway for the individual to withdraw from the group and to carry on schemes of play without interruption. We find that quite intensive social play, like ball throwing or hauling each other in wagons, seems to reach a point of spontaneous disintegration. Without coming to a climax, it subsides, and is usually followed by a period of quiet during which each child is employed at some individual activity such as play in sand or pebbles, block building, or work at the bench. Throughout the nursery school age this characteristic remains typical of the children. It is one that should be encouraged since it protects them from the strain of sustaining too long periods of accommodation to the demands of close social contact.

It is important for us all to learn to get on in our social groups, to find ourselves at home with other people, to make the concessions demanded by harmonious social living. It is quite as essential that we each make a contribution to the group in which we find ourselves, and at its richest that contribution is in terms of constructive ideas and stimulation, not merely of social charm.

Frances could usually affect her group. She could call the children from their self-initiated occupations and engage them in elaborate dramatizations. The group and her power over them seemed to stimulate her, but their role was always kept a passive one. There was never a constructive impulse given to the group play or that of individual members by her association with them; and as in the course of time their own interests deepened, they were able to resist her bids for their attention. The teacher's effort was turned toward providing opportunities for Frances to develop individual play schemes so that her dramatizations would be worked out with materials rather than as pure fantasies.

Another child, Leonore, seemed to have an equal power over her mates; but the play she initiated controlled them less and seemed to give them an impulse toward further play. A train-journey dramatization was likely to begin with blocks, and each child who joined her would contribute from his own experience, the play becoming fuller in incident but less closely knit as a social scheme. It was at the same time a more appropriate and a more fruitful type of activity than that which evolved through Frances' more sophisticated and probably maturer method.

Frances' ideas were not really shared; they were apparently too diffused and too little formulated for her to communicate them to her mates. Furthermore, her interest seemed to be in controlling the other children and limiting the scope of their activities. Leonore's dramatic conceptions were concrete, requiring material properties as well as a cast. Her attention was on the content rather than on the control of her company, and any member who could bring further elaboration to the plot found ample opportunity for his prowess. In other words, the social element of the play was not the most important one.

I define Frances' method as more mature, but it was so only in her ability to appreciate the extent of her power to control other children. Real maturity, however, should mean integration of one's powers: the maintenance of equilibrium under a variety of conditions. When the situation called for adaptation on her part to a group activity, Frances withdrew; and these were the two "lessons" that the nursery school had to teach her: to join in group-initiated activity as a subordinate member, if need be, and to lose herself in a productive individual occupation. When she grows up to her social impulse, it will probably mean real power instead of exploitation of the younger or less dynamic children about her. . . .

. . . What can most effectively give children emotional release so that they can let go the "ties that bind" them too closely to infantile satisfactions?

We believe it is play, for play gives them opportunities for the expenditure of energy and, by the nature of the materials provided, gives them increasing control of their bodies—skill in handling themselves and material. Through play, and again by the nature of the materials provided, children can represent situations and processes that have interested them: can recall details, can rehearse (and in the process, create), can invent and construct to the extent of such resources as are theirs at any given period. When play involves living in a social community, they gain the joys of companionship, of building up a common fund of experiences together, of uniting in play schemes, and of gaining the ability to make the concessions necessary in such a situation,—even of suffering the frustrations inherent in a life that is shared with other demanding persons. . . .

*A child can comprehend relations readily when
his experience is kept real and simple*

. . . Besides providing play materials, the nursery
school must give its children experiences from age to
age which shall have continuity and relationship, so
that the field of operation, the horizon which bounds
the child's world, will be gradually and logically
widened. In this way he will acquire the habit of
looking at the phenomena about him not as discrete
objects and events but as related or contributing
factors in other features of his life. The teacher who,
after grumbling for years over the debris of a New
York street on the edge of a recent subway construction, was heard to remark that the city was crim-
inally dilatory in its program of street repair gives a
classic example of the uninquisitive mind that does
not attempt to relate phenomena. A four-year-old,
on the other hand, handed her dinner plate to the
maid who was washing the dishes, then turned at
once to the teacher and said, "Her hands are *hot*."
The teacher said, "Why do you suppose they are?"
The child began, "The little stove . . ." hesitated in
evident thought, then said, "The little stove in the
cellar is making the water hot, and that's why."
Though she had been taken to see the hot water
heater, she had not previously perceived this particular connection. . . .

The nursery school has been called a child's world.

Its chief worth lies in the fact that in it children's occupations can be appreciated at their real value because they are the serious business of the community. In the family, however deeply concerned its members are with the children and their activities and play, the adult business of earning a livelihood, of administering a household, of study or recreation, takes precedence. In a research center a child of five reported to his mother one night, "I didn't have time to do my work today because I had to be measured so much." That seriousness about his own undertakings is gained as much from the adults' attitudes as from the child's native sense of the importance of his own work.

However, the nursery world must have its contacts with the life outside; its object must be to help the child to find his place there and to understand its affairs, or it fails of its purpose.

For a time the home or the nursery school holds all that a child needs. Finding his way about, learning the uses of things, identifying and placing his own and other children's belongings, and reproducing in play the experiences that he has had so far, are orienting him little by little into life as it is in the world of reality. His interest soon begins to extend beyond these narrow confines into the outside environment. His introduction to this world should be so made that he will hold the thread of a familiar experience as he goes out to gain a new one. A fact has no value in and of itself; the significance of one experience or fact lies in its relationship to others.

A child may see trains of cars for years without appreciating the human needs which they serve, and with no understanding of a connection between them and the coal that comes for his mother's cooking stove or the fruit that a neighbor sends to the distant city. He may play milkman with no understanding of the processes by which the farm and milk stations in the city are related. It really matters little through what sort of experience this process of thinking in terms of relationships begins. During the nursery school period it takes an extremely simplified form, but the attempt is made to maintain a continuity in the experiences offered children and to see that it has a definite relationship to their play schemes. When trips outside the school are well developed, there results from them a marked enrichment of the play that is carried on and the work with paints, crayons, or clay, also shows that the children have gained in expressive powers.

Play activities then take on a renewed significance, for by means of them a child can rehearse and reproduce the parts of his experience which have significance for him: he dramatizes processes which have interested him and catches some rhythm or pattern in form or color, which gives him the creative joy of the artist.

Social relationships also become more active and important, more closely knit, and more truly social; for cooperative effort grows with maturing powers, and a child must have ideas and the ability to execute them if he is to gain power in the nursery school commonwealth.

*Trips for children need to be planned toward continuity and relevance of experience*

. . . I believe that it is important that the educational process be made a continuous one. By this I do not mean that we should make sure that at the end of their nursery school career there is a kindergarten ready for the babies to step into. I mean that we must assure children a continuity in experiences, so that as they go on they not only find that the world is so full of a number of things but develop an expectation that there are connections between some of these things, at least, and have a dim notion of what some of those connections are in relation to their own living. This cannot be, unless the persons planning the program have a clearer idea than the children of what relationships and connections they are trying to establish. What are some of the things that we feel it is important for nursery school children to be realizing and experiencing? They have come into a world which is humming along on its own power. As far as the little child is concerned, it is humming about him as a center. The place of other people—after he has learned that they aren't other manifestations of Me but are independent, operating within their own spheres—he has got to learn. Many things about him which have to do in various ways with him, his welfare, his pleasure and his needs, are unknown to him.

His place in this world, his relations to other people, what people have done to their world and what it has yielded them, how he can affect the environment and by what means: aren't these the most important beginnings of wisdom that we can give him? Another way of saying it would be: he must learn to find his way about, to orient himself in his environment; and while getting a sense of an orderly procession of events, must gain the power of directing himself through them. Still another way of saying it would be to call it by a grand name, like an introduction to economics or human geography or social science.

What can he take as he proceeds from stage to stage? By what means will he gain power, control, and clarity, in his thinking?

First, it seems to me, by simplicity in the environment we plan. Let us not have too many pieces of material, either in actual numbers or in variety. Let us put our emphasis upon what is sometimes called raw material: that is, upon things which become significant in the hands of the children. An elaborate train on a track, a doll house with equipment, a toy village or mechanical toy, are not examples. Blocks, boards, crayons, are.

Let us try to let children have the opportunity to play out fully the experiences through which they have lived, before we add more. When we do lead them on, let it be to something which has some already known features. For instance, if children are playing with toy horses, a visit to a stable is more constructive than a trip to the zoo would be. Let us try not to have too wide a variety in the kinds of life about them that we assign for exploration. There is much in any environment which they can wait to understand; let us choose features with which they already have some connections. What people eat, and how they get it; how people get about and by what means; where people stay when they are at home; where trains stay when they are at home, and animals, and boats; all these are subjects which appeal equally to the country and to the city child, and which have vital and easily recognizable connections.

. . . The experiences through which children live are the stuff of which their dramatic play is made. Most children soon learn to regard the play materials as an essential part of their play; and as their social life develops, their interest in cooperative schemes also grows. We find their early play adventures to be concerned with details of their own personal care and their share in the domestic life. Children explain all phenomena in terms of their own experience. The sun under a cloud is the moon, at two years; smoke coming from a distant chimney may be a boat to a three-year-old. We need not be disturbed by such inaccuracies, for the process of testing out their observations goes on tirelessly till truth emerges.

It must always be remembered that children's range of experience must be widened if their interest is to be held. As they grow older, they snatch from such a casual experience as their train journey to the country, from a visit to the seashore, or from a ferry-boat excursion, certain outstanding details. If we, whether we are parents or teachers, could be aware of the lines of interest thus aroused and could open them up more fully, we should be amazed at the impulse that is given to children's play. By this I mean, give them opportunities to find out at first hand more about these places or things or processes. They will return to adaptable play materials with new zest and devise new ways of using them. We must remember always that we are living in a culture that is overwhelmingly complex, and that the only possible method of simplification is to limit experience primarily to what a child can get at first hand. His stage of development will depend not only upon his age but also upon the opportunities for experience he has had and upon how these experiences have been treated by the adults about him.

The technique of introducing children to further experience in their environment by taking trips cannot be considered in detail at this point; but in general there are certain procedures that are effective. Take the child to see something with which he already has made some acquaintance either by casual encounter or on an earlier trip. Restrict your own interests to that object or process or place so that there will be as little distraction as possible. If you go to a railway yard, do not allow yourself to be diverted by a dock on the way. If the child's interest is normally keen, let him take his own time and choose the details he wants to look at. He may for a long time pay no attention to the things that you most anticipate his discovering. Repeat the same trip so that later the children can feel a thorough intimacy with the activities which they wish to reproduce. They feel a special enjoyment in the recognition of familiar features. Have a time set aside for talking over the trip, making sure that as many children as possible make verbal the images they have formed. In this discussion the teacher will try to encourage the recall in sense and motor terms, a method to which children are always responsive but which they do not use unless a sample is given them.

Six-year-old children were asked to pretend that they were something that they had felt or seen or heard or smelled or touched. After a ferry-boat trip across New York harbor came this: "I splash up on the sides and make a long white streak behind." After a visit to a farm: "If I were a little calf, I'd have a split in my toes." A cannon made an impression upon one child, who said, "Iron is my long strong throat."

It is to be remembered that accurate information is only one feature of the experience. Information gathered in the course of one's own activity seems really valid and important. A sensitivity to the details of sight and sound and feeling and the capacity to recall through language symbols are of equal value.

The results may be reckoned in various ways: by the habits of observation and of interest in the environment which are built up; by the increase in mental activity and in power to think through a situation; by the ingenuity and inventiveness developed through adapting materials to representative use; and, most important by far, by the stimulus that is given to the art-play of children, and the resulting pleasure and satisfaction.

The teacher's job is not to prepare for a future of purposeful activities but to recognize the age levels in children's interests and to make sure that at every level their powers are being used as fully and as purposefully as possible.

In this connection, we need a definition of the word purpose. We too often think of it as meaning an act which is worthwhile from an adult's point of view, or as involving planning beforehand. If a young child refuses to accept an adult's ruling and rebels with all the strength and all the guile that is in him, we do sometimes use a synonym for purposeful to describe his behavior and say that he is determined, though we also call him difficult or disobedient, but do we often say, "What a purposeful youngster he is!" When a two-year-old refuses help and walks a plank or negotiates the stairs alone, his purpose is just as strong, and his object just as praiseworthy, as that of a student struggling with arithmetic or working out the problem of a mitered joint in shop. Purpose and purposeful activities cannot be postponed to a kindergarten or first grade. If the children in a nursery school are not acquiring habits of work that are applicable to life situations outside its walls, if their activities lack the buoyancy and the affective spontaneity and fire of purpose, the adults responsible for the school have to answer the grave charge of wasting children's time. The younger the child, the more difficult for a grown-up to understand his purpose; but there is a dynamic quality to genuine play, there is an affective response to a good life, which can always be recognized by the discriminating, and at any age. . . .

### The teacher's role is distinct from that of the parent

. . . In certain respects the teacher's role is more advantageous than that of the parent. The teacher, like the parent, is working to effect certain objectives; but she has the child working with her. She has based her program upon certain interests and tendencies she has observed in children and found to be favorable to growth. She does not fail to establish herself as a person of authority in the group, but the business of school lies largely in the hands of the children. The equipment is comparatively limited, but the use of what we provide is open to the children and free for them to choose. There is not the usual compulsion.

That is, there is no implication in the attitude of the teacher that *she* has set up standards of conduct and that *she* as a person exacts compliance with them. It is rather that she and the children are members of a community, where certain things are done or not done. Offenses against social conventions or good taste, or against adult dignity are not brought to the conscious attention of the children. They are distinctly a part of the teacher's consideration, but her method of dealing with them is quite opposed to that used by the world toward children. It is more comparable to that used in adult society. She attempts to establish a program of social living; and her emphasis is quite consistently, I believe, upon behavior that makes for general good.

Routine is carried along as inevitably as it is at home; perhaps even more so, for the exceptions to the rule that one always finds amazingly frequent when one is called upon to chart one's own child's program do not happen—cannot happen—in a school. It is not the teacher's decision that makes dinner appear or that can defer or omit morning lunch or afternoon nap. I believe that this may be one reason why school routine is so much more easily applied than home routine. It—and by this I mean not only the program but also the intimate procedures—is actually more objective. We cannot, even if we wish, ignore or combat or overcome the strength of the emotional tie between child and parents. The silver cord remains, but it may be shackles or it may be a fine electric wire over which may run messages of understanding, of real communication, at the wish or discretion or decision of the holders of the receiving apparatus at either end.

The sort of sensitiveness that parent and child have for each other is not, thank God, present in the teacher-child relationship. The good teacher, the best teacher, while remaining a human being, has one general problem before her: that of making sure that in this child world each child is freed for as complete living as his resources allow. Temper tantrums, an excessive drive for adult attention, anxiety, timidity, are blocks in the way of integrated growth. They threaten present serenity and future development. A whole gamut of feelings that may overwhelm a parent only remotely concerns the teacher. Humiliation felt by the parent because his child makes a poor impression when he really is such an unusual person; irritation because he complicates life at the moments when it is already so febrile that anything more cannot be endured; resentment because his behavior is showing one up as a poor parent: all these trials are distinctly parental ones. "Good" and "bad" in the usual sense are hardly in the vocabulary of the ideal teacher. Good as it relates to personality development and to the development of group living is her deep concern. About such good she is stirred and moved overwhelmingly; but the action she takes is to strengthen and free the child's interest and activity and establish him in a satisfactory relationship with his group, rather than to urge conformity to an acceptable pattern of behavior.

*The teacher's control is a function of her combined skill and understanding*

Teacher control in the classroom is a misleading term. We mean by it a variety of things: first, perhaps, the methods that are used when some details of the program are resisted by the children or when the teacher-child or child-child relationship is in question; and second, those that keep the program moving, that add an experience when it is needed, that make it possible for a curriculum to have meaning and unity in terms of child control.

Specifically, what is the procedure when dinner is refused, when nap is resisted, not only passively but violently and at the expense of group serenity? What should the teacher's reaction be to personal attacks, and how does her response differ with different age levels? What should she do about flagrant social violations—biting, seizing toys, pushing? At what point shall she enter the play situation to check or to stimulate?

As I see it, the basis of indecision in regard to these things rests on the assumption traditionally held that teachers were not people in their relationship with children. They were guides and counsellors but never friends. They were guardians of morals, they were fountains of wisdom, they had a very active instructional attitude and responsibility toward their pupils, and always they were persons above and apart.

Then came the new education, and the pendulum swung out into a different arc—if such a figure can mean anything. Preschool education was taken very seriously, especially in the larger research centers. The Child, capitalized, was to be regarded with such respect that no adult was to intrude upon his activities or his impulses. He was permitted experimentation and investigation, in the course of which he would develop habits, attitudes, and skills, which would help him become a self-educated social being. The role of the teacher was to be that of the benevolent neutral, an automaton, all of whose reactions would be so studied and so controlled that no personal flavor except approval or disapproval could reach the children.

A third point of view seems to us more nearly an approach to normal. Here are children and adults living in a social group. The attitude of the adults, the teachers, is that the society established is essentially the children's. The activities carried on are child-initiated, and freedom from dependence on adults is one of the major aims; yet there must be a relationship between teacher and children which is as genuine to the adults as it is to the children.

This creates the possibility of spontaneous social responses on the part of the teachers. That is, as soon as the teacher ceases to be a detached superior and becomes the senior partner in a social organization, she has less fear about just what response she should make in any given situation. The moment she becomes assured, she is a freer and therefore a more easily understood person. From that point on she tries to examine conclusions and to determine the degree to which her own individual prejudices or points of view have weighted her planning. To a certain and limited extent this is possible; but for the most part, her safest course is again to go back to children: to their early growth tendencies, to their responses to the curriculum, and to observable steps in their development. . . .

. . . Above and beyond the practical techniques of

classroom teaching, of planning trips, discussions, and stories, so that the sense of continuity which the teacher feels will be communicated to the children in terms of an ordered living and experiencing together, there are other methods used by the skilled teacher which lend to the life of the group a lyric quality of beauty and joy. It is true that each teacher has an opportunity to use in her teaching whatever individual artistry is native to her in her contacts with people.

It may take the form of a bantering, humorous response. A child catching the word "please" says with a grin, "Did you ever hear of 'ease'?" "Did you ever hear of 'tease'?" counters the teacher promptly. "Did you ever hear of 'ice'?" laughs Henry. "Did you ever hear of 'mice'?" the teacher flashes back companionably.

It may take the form of whole-hearted appreciation of a joke, even one directed against the authority of the teacher. It may mean that in a quiet moment between items in the schedule the teacher will recall something the group has done or seen together, a sensuous rather than an intellectual experience. "Do you remember how the snow bent down the branches of the big pine tree when you were playing snow-birds under it last week?"

It may mean the adaptation of an expression in some story or poem they have all enjoyed together. In a tense moment among six-year-olds, an explanation concluding with a cheerful, "And so that was all right, Best Beloved," from their favorite "Just So Stories" cleared away the clouds at once. . . .

. . . The first attention of the teacher is directed to knowing and understanding the individual children and introducing herself to them so that they will know and understand her. The younger the children, the more all adults seem alike to them. They are likely to address all teachers as "mama"; and after they get the name of one, to apply it to all: "Louise," "other Louise," just as all children, including themselves, are "baby."

The relationship which the teacher has to establish is different from that which the child has known before. It is less indulgent and less demonstrative; but at the same time personal, intimate, and attentive. Her attitude is equally authoritative but less corrective. She is working all the time to make children independent of her, to teach them to look to themselves for the solution of their problems; but at the same time she has and maintains a real place in the social group. She is never a neutral spectator.

It is a very intensive individual study that she is undertaking, for however important the group concerns are, the individual members must not be allowed to sink out of notice. With little children there may be personality problems which have already assumed serious proportions, like acute fears, or muscle tensions, or a fixation on familiar adults, which make adjustment an acute and also an imperative item for consideration and treatment. Some of these difficulties might not be discovered, if the teacher were not holding in mind the opportunities offered the children in the school situation and each child's acceptance or rejection of them. Children are allowed, for instance, a wide choice in their activities; but if one of them consistently avoids heights, or consistently limits his play to vehicles which keep him seated while propelled or propelling, it becomes part of the teacher's challenge and satisfaction to free him from restricting fears and narrowing choices so that he may meet his environment with the zest of confidence. . . .

. . . Teachers as well as children must proceed from the point which they have reached in their understanding. They must go from the known to fields of further investigation. It is still a much debated question, how far teachers should be expected to enter the mental hygiene field. It seems to me somewhat comparable to that of physical health. We ask teachers to be students of behavior; to be so aware of the usual responses of children that they can detect variations in individual patterns and from them can judge whether a child is in a state of health which makes it advisable for him to remain in the group, to be withdrawn for a period of rest, or to be excluded for his own safety and that of other children. We do not expect teachers to diagnose or to treat illness, but to judge when a physician should be consulted or responsibility turned back to the home.

I realize that the critical difference between physical and mental health, from the viewpoint of the teacher, lies in the fact that the educational program may contribute to the treatment of disturbed emotional states to a greater extent than it does to the treatment of any specific physical disorder. As far as general hygiene is concerned, the school program should contribute to physical and mental health alike, and we believe that within and because of the school experiences our children gain in physical vigor, in emotional control, in buoyancy and satisfaction, unless they are suffering from serious maladjustments. Ability to recognize symptoms requiring more expert help than it lies in the school's power to give should certainly be a part of the teacher's equipment.

Beyond that there is a job that is essentially the teacher's: namely, that of working out the principles on which she bases her educational procedures, planning the experiences which are to be offered children, and building up the methods by which, as children gain in maturity, continuity is to be maintained so that the school's program becomes an integrated one. To do this, she must know something of the activities and interests which engage children and how these activities and interests change with increasing maturity: the maturity levels of different growth periods. She must go a step further before her researches can serve her in their practical application to the educational process. She will find impulses that tend to pull children back into familiar, well-trodden paths of dependence as well as those that promise experience on a wider horizon. She will find the cultivation of limiting, restricting activities less difficult, often, than those which tend to establish a child in a more dynamic relationship to his environment. She will observe that reliance upon her or upon other members of the group may seem to give deeper satisfaction than does self-initiation. However, from the wide variety of behavior patterns that she observes, she must choose those which seem most surely to favor development, and must cultivate them by means of the play materials she provides and the attitudes she holds toward the activities carried on by the children.

Teaching I conceive to be continually a learning situation. It is essential that the teacher construct a hypothesis, a conception of the conditions within which children can live together and grow most profitably, and that she carry out a program consistent with her conception. However, she will maintain a critical attitude toward the program and her educational practice, and will attempt to test it by the new knowledge of children and of growth that the extension of her experience brings her. There must be stability in the school environment and consistency in the methods used with children. It takes time to test any thesis. An experimental attitude does not mean rapid shifts in method. It implies clear-eyed honesty in looking at one's work and a willingness to make modifications which will hold it truer to its original purpose.

The teacher is a specialist in education. She has before her the task of building a curriculum, and of testing its suitability and effectiveness with the group as well as in the case of individual children. It is essential that she work closely with other specialists concerned with the problems of growth, especially in the field of emotional motivation, and that she gain enough insight into the basis of their assumptions to understand their possible relationship to her work. . . .

### The progressive teacher requires progressive training

. . . Why is there so much agitation just now about teachers of progressive schools? In educational conferences and periodicals one hears addresses and reads articles discussing at length the demands made on teachers by the newer education but rarely the opportunities and privileges it opens to them.

The teacher needs first of all to *see* children. She needs to see them primarily as active doers: to understand that at all ages doing is a force for growing, if it is controlled and directed by the individual in action; she needs to study the impulses that dominate children at different periods and to recognize whether their drive is native or results from adult influence. Second, she needs to realize children's powers, the scope of their ability to handle problems, whether concerned with everyday living or more narrowly intellectual. Third, she needs to appreciate that children are essentially artists and that it is the process of the creative use of materials rather than the resulting product that is important in growth.

Beyond all this, she needs to have resources at her command so that she can sustain an experimental attitude toward the work she is doing and can be ready to regard the opinions she holds as subject to change if her own growth or further experiences lead her to modify them. It is this that makes teaching a continuous learning process. It is not a matter of fixed knowing but of finding out.

How can a teacher learn these things more vividly than by living in an environment which opens to her opportunities to test her own powers, to pursue lines of investigation in various fields, to try out for herself some form of art expression?

In our schools the exploration of the environment is done in terms of the level of maturity and interest in each age group. We find that the process itself at each age means a distinct sharpening of children's observation, an increase in the ability to seize upon salient points, and an added enjoyment in living and playing. The same thing seems to be true of adults. Crossing the ferry with a group of teachers who have done field work in their own environment reveals the value of their experience. One gets a sense that the world is an open source book and the study of it a thrilling adventure.

This is only an illustration of a method of teacher training which we believe would begin to make teachers more real and vivid people, better able to give the newer education the security and stability of the older formal method, without losing the poignancy and delight of a creative art.

The child who, meeting her teacher, said, "I thought at first you were a lady," was making a distinction that has often been made in thought if not in speech, not that teachers have not been considered ladies but that they have not been expected to be real people. It is essentially the real person that the modern school requires: a person who has had richness and variety in her background, to whom life has brought developing experience aside from the scholastic training required by her school job.

The same methods prevail when the teachers lead their pupils back into the past or afar into distant fields. The modern school asks of teachers a quality that is rarer than encyclopedic knowledge of a subject. They must see their particular field in its relation to various situations and times. They must be familiar with source materials so that whether the question that comes up concerns certain modern processes in manufacture or political life in the time of the Incas, they can open up significant lines of investigation for pupils to follow, and can suggest points of discussion which will lead students to see the bearing of one phase of modern life upon other phases or to find common factors in ancient and more recent periods of history.

The people of this present-day culture tend to live vicariously to an extent beyond that of any previous age. They look at other people's work and play; they listen to other people speak or sing; they satisfy their interest in games by watching a score board or listening to a radio announcer. We are not entirely complacent about this tendency. We become restless and seek a more active sharing in life.

There seem to be two methods used by people as a compensation and resistance to this sort of living. The first is an attempt to divert the vicarious experience of the present to an equally vicarious but less feverish living in the past. A study of past civilizations when they were in the process of growth seems a more significant experience to many persons than any sort of study of or participation in our own. The art of the past is more alive, because more familiar and better understood, than present experiments in new forms. Primitive processes seem more full of meaning to these scholarly protestants than any achievement of this mechanistic age.

The second method involves using the here and now, looking at the past in the light of the present and at both as phases in an evolutionary process which is still going on. Its emphasis is on the future rather than the past. The group which is its exponent demands participation in the present. They seek avenues of exploration. They repudiate the role of quiescent acceptance and raise questions which they attempt to answer by their own investigations. They tend to undertake a wide field of experimentation, with the result that their activities seem perhaps cruder and their techniques often less masterly than those of the first group.

Which of these methods means an actual grappling with present conditions? Will social progress and maturity ever come by a retreat from reality? If we are ever to cope with the evils of the present age and if we are ever fully to profit by its advantages, we must face it and understand it.

We can never turn back the clock and revert to a period of simpler, less sophisticated living. Evolution does not proceed that way; and after all, the normal person in any day and age is the one who faces life and lives it, trying at least to get the drift of the tendencies of his times, to understand them. This, it seems to me, is the basis of modern school planning.

To carry on such education, teachers are needed: more of the rare spirits that the fortunate among us may have met once or twice in the course of our school years. In his recent book a schoolman, Abraham Flexner, quite unintentionally stated the case for the progressive school in these words: "From the standpoint of practical need, society requires of its leaders not so much specifically trained competency at the moment, as the mastery of experience, an interest in problems, dexterity in finding one's way, disciplined capacity to put forth effort." When opportunities for growth are found within the educational field, it will be possible to attract to training schools teachers who have the qualities for such leadership; and the challenge of the children will be answered.

. . . In planning a good educational environment, consideration should be given to the fact that there is a high degree of instability in the home in this day and age, due in part to the difficulty of maintaining economic stability and in part to the fact that the family status is changing. Often this means a serious feeling of insecurity on the part of the children.

The nursery school in many cases represents an anchor to windward, a place that the child finds unchanged in a changing and kaleidoscopic world. *There* is found security, because the place and program are sustained, and consistency (a virtue in and of itself) in treatment, in values, in standards, is maintained and can be relied upon. The nursery school must be this sort of place.

As a part of the process of establishing a child in a feeling of security and satisfaction, there is also the break from dependence upon parents and nurses. The nursery school is especially fitted to carry on a psychological weaning process, because its informality and intimacy make possible an interim of acquaintance and adjustment on a home level before independence is expected or established.

The traits that are unfavorable to personality development are much more easily treated in a group; first, because we all tend to do what is being done by our friends and, second, because the good teacher is not disturbed for moral reasons by deviation from desired conduct. She thinks not of what is good or bad but of what is, in the situation before her, good or bad for this particular individual. Her treatment is not colored by personal bias nor by the emotional feeling of responsibility which a parent has for the character traits of the child concerned. . . .

*The child's security can be protected in the face of new situations and undertakings*

. . . We have tried to make the set-up like a home in its informality and intimacy, and unlike it in that it is planned to serve children's activities rather than adults' occupations. We have attempted to plan an environment that unmistakably stamps itself as belonging to children. We have subordinated adult furnishings and belongings, reducing them to the minimum equipment necessary for record keeping and for getting meals. We have also in this process subordinated prettiness and grace in our surroundings. In the child's nursery of the department store or the woman's magazine, planning for children is effected solely by a reduction in scale. Low-set gay curtained cupboards, low-hung pictures, decorated walls, gay paint, and small-scale furniture do the trick. We have, on the contrary, quite deliberately left bare spaces and emptiness. Small-scale furniture, toys accessible on low shelves, and apparatus for full-body activities are in evidence in our nursery; but we have sacrificed decorative features wherever they might make for confusion or would mean restriction on the children's initiative.

The home into which a baby comes is a going concern, with the affairs of the family already organized and in operation at his advent. The home is planned for adults to live in. It may have been founded largely for the rearing of children, but babyhood is, after all, a small part of life, and there are adults in a family before and after there are children. Moreover, the care of children as well as the needs of adults require a set-up which is essentially adult-planned and adult-managed. In these days of congestion and small incomes the needs of the majority must be considered first. If children have separate sleeping rooms and a play space of their own, they are unusually favored. The baby is, then, more or less of an outsider in the environment waiting to receive him.

Before the runabout age, food, sleep and change of position are the chief essentials and are well met, for the most part, in the well regulated home. Education on the physical needs of babies has taken long strides ahead through the public health centers, with their prenatal work and baby clinics.

The development of the emotional life is another story. There is hardly need to review the habits which the nursery school finds already set up in the affective life of normal, young children. The baby is quite literally the center of the household. Even if this is not so as far as the interests of the parents are concerned, provision is made so that no household exigencies are allowed to interfere with his schedule. We boast that not heat nor cold, earthquake nor sudden death, has ever caused the omission of the ten-thirty orange juice. Admirable as this precision is, it may carry with it an unfortunate emotional implication. The infant lives in a world of Olympians, but they are his willing slaves, even in the most normal home and among parents whose emotional life is well balanced. When, however, he begins extending the sphere of his activities, he meets new conditions. He finds new and alluring materials, new possibilities for experimentation, and encounters as well the incessant "Don't" or "Not for baby," which lie inherent in the situation. Questions of danger to his life and limb and of destruction of property cramp his style and quench the ardor of his adventuring spirit.

Parents try to meet this difficulty in one of several ways, or sometimes in each of several ways in succession. With freedom for the individual as a watchword, they turn over the adult living quarters to the children, reducing themselves to cramped space, presently to realize that adults are also individuals and that tranquillity among them is essential also to the happiness of younger members of the household. Or they may try to limit the child to his own small quarters, with only brief supervised and directed excursions into Olympia. The third experiment, which is the most usual, is to allow the child to share the house, with plenty of his own possessions about, and to depend upon patient and logical training to teach him mine and thine.

A child finds, then, in the beginning of his career, his impulses toward the free exercise of his newly found physical powers cramped and restricted. He is apt to turn the investigation of his environment from the inanimate materials which are forbidden, to the human material which is constantly at hand. It is less well adapted to his needs, because it is not stable in its reactions. He is, of course, sure of a response; and the intensity of his interest depends upon the quality of the reaction he gets. It does not, however, depend solely upon whether or not it is pleasant. If it is also intense, it holds him.

The tables and chairs, the china and mirrors, present a certain limited range of possibilities. Given a definite method of treatment, one can with certitude expect a certain predictable response. It is quite different with human material: mothers, fathers, nurses, cooks. The child pursues with admirable courage and patience a trial-and-error method, but the factors of mood and of fatigue which enter into his relationships are so far beyond his analysis that the pursuit never ends in an acquired skill or technique except one for getting a reaction. A cart on an incline, or a tower of blocks, presents a problem which may be learned; but mother on Friday night after a week of hard work or nurse after a Thursday quarrel with her best young man is quite different from mother or nurse in a melting mood. Materials lead a child on in inquiry and in the acquisition of more and more skill in a given performance. Human beings may develop in him capacities for the diplomatic service, but that hardly falls in with what we know of the needs of growth for the preschool child.

What I have sketched here may seem an exaggeration, but everyone recognizes the picture in modified form. We find it varying from that of the child who carries on vigorous play if his mother's attention is always on tap for him, to one who is physically inactive and dependent for his satisfaction upon actual physical contact with his mother or one who is positively anti-social, refusing to be intrigued by other children or by play material. I have purposely omitted the grossly abnormal child.

Without definite plan the nursery school environment differs from the home in its emotional quality. Persons whose chief interest is in an objective study of children are unlikely to have an emotional attitude toward them. Furthermore, the nursery group has some of the advantages of the large family. No one baby can hold the center of the stage all the time. The situation itself has this to offer; but besides, our set-up is planned. The situations that confront the children are, for the most part, intentional; and our procedure with them, while it is experimental in the sense of being tentative and not dogmatic, is a thought-out procedure. Faulty it may often be, because it is of necessity based upon the theory and experience which colors the attitude of the staff who share the children's lives. It is not, however, colored by a personal intimate relationship nor by a sense of responsibility or of fatalism such as a parent often feels when he sees his own qualities manifested in his offspring. We have not the retreat of the parents,

"He did not get that trait from my side of the family."

I am trying to show that the atmosphere of the nursery school is objective, not that it is impersonal. We believe that the babies should find in the new environment a genuine personal welcome. We wish to make it possible for the children and the adults to form real relationships. A part of their social experience comes to them through contacts with varying personalities and their adjustments to them.

In life outside the school the individuals with whom a child comes into more or less intimate contact are as widely different as the grandparents, with their long past experience as a background, the modern parents trying to work out newly acquired theories, and the maid or nurse, who, left with much responsibility and no authority, tries to steer a course which will "let her by" in safety. Do we know anything about the confusion in a child's mind over the varying attitudes he sees taken by the adults about him toward similar phenomena? In the nursery there are different personalities, but we try to maintain consistency, if not uniformity, in our treatment of situations. . . .

We must remember that nursery babies on arrival have not yet perfected their powers of locomotion. They are quite able to get about, so that they are making contacts far beyond the boundaries of the infant's reach; but they are often hardly more than launched in the adventure of walking. Wide free spaces to explore; possibilities for climbing, stepping over obstacles, pulling, hauling, and lifting; materials to be investigated: these are to a child what a well equipped laboratory is to an eager scientist and even the dependent child turns from adults for experimentation down such paths.

On the other hand, these same paths lead him, head on, toward social contacts with his peers for which he is ill prepared. In the early months this means little to many babies. There seems to be a sort of generalized, diffused awareness and enjoyment of other children, but little assertiveness. Later in most cases, the gamut is run, through aggressiveness and attack to social playing together (playing with similar materials at the same time), finally emerging into true cooperative play, a joint effort toward a common purpose. Such a consummation is not attained without fundamental adjustments and attendant strain. Whether the strain is commensurate with the developing powers of children of nursery age is one of the questions we must ask ourselves.

One cannot fling babies into the maelstrom of a self-determined physical existence and a collective life, and then stand coolly back to watch the results and applaud the survivors. The ordinary home places gates at the head of the stairs not with the determination to bar out a dangerous experience from its child's life but in order that he may have time to learn under supervision the difficulties of that sort of descent, before he hurls himself down to his destruction. So in the nursery we are at hand not to reduce adventure but to ensure children safety in their experimentation during the initial stages. We know what the effect of fear is in building up aversions as we know what the effect of success is in the acquisition of beneficial habits. We try not to hold children back in their experiments with their bodies and with the physical environment; but in really perilous undertakings we attempt to ensure them safety. Also, in cases of disaster we encourage an immediate return to the unsuccessful undertaking, and persistence in it till the feeling of insecurity or reluctance has worked off. I do not mean that we introduce children to pieces of apparatus that they do not seek, nor that we urge them over a reluctance; but that, once they have adventured and failed, we encourage another immediate trial.

In the same way we attempt to safeguard their social experimentation until they have become somewhat oriented. It is a radical venture we are carrying on when we undertake to rear children in litters; for though the age range is small, individual differences even below two make children unequal opponents. We feel that the introduction to group life should come very slowly; in the first place, because we believe that experimentation with the physical environment is more profitable than with human material, and in the second, because there must develop out of social experience a social technique, if success is to crown our efforts to live together. A technique of a sort would probably result if we let our youngsters explore the possibilities of their contacts with each other without our intervention; but we believe that a problem which in its complexities has proved baffling to so many of us would demand from them too great an expense of nervous energy in meeting it. Therefore we do try to protect the children from each other at first, to mitigate the force of personal encounters, and to lead the children's attention to play materials. We also attempt to give them little by little the "rules of the game," which develop very logically out of the group situation and are applicable alike to all members of it. Such rules are that toys are owned in common; possession is established by use; apparatus must be used in turns; pushing and personal violence mean removal from the group. We believe that experience in this sort of living makes the children more ready and able participants in the world beyond nursery doors.

# PART III

Notes on the Study of Individual Children in
a School Situation

*A Study of One Child's Immature Response*

*to the Nursery School Environment*

*A Developmental Comparison of Two Children*

*of the Same Age*

## EDITORIAL NOTE

WE CANNOT emphasize too greatly the fact that Harriet Johnson planned and conducted an educational experiment. Each tentative conclusion required checking. Techniques for checking experiments in education are young and baffling. The recording of behavior, in one form or another, is the chief source for accumulating data. For reasons which have been referred to in the first chapter of this book, Harriet Johnson and her staff chose to take the major body of their behavior records in diary form, having established and expressed the criteria for the selection of behavior items to be recorded. They were intent upon building up a body of vital, objective data on how children behave in the course of growing up and were unwilling to make obeisance to that definition of objectivity which would have all records meet the requirements of detailed statistical analysis.

The records upon which the following papers were based were part of a study of growth conducted by the Bureau of Educational Experiments which included physical examinations, X-rays of arm, hand and wrist, X-rays of chest and heart, electrocardiograms, psychometric examinations, and family histories. The use made of the behavior records in relation to these other measurements is not discussed here. The use made of them by Harriet Johnson, herself, in the interest of testing out what they contributed to the understanding of individual children, is illustrated in the studies which follow. The records incorporated are of two kinds: first, the direct behavior record recounting in detail what the recorder observed as she observed it; second, the summary account of a phase of behavior based on the direct records.

In fairness it seems important to note that what follow are not the complete studies as they were presented by Miss Johnson. Space does not permit the inclusion of all the records which she used as evidence for indicating any trend in growth. It has been necessary to select certain records to illustrate her points in lieu of including the complete series by means of which it was her habit to support her statements. Furthermore, publication of these studies was never Miss Johnson's intention. The pages which follow are the working sheets through which she constructed her picture of a child. These working notes were used some years ago as the basis for reports to the Bureau staff, and proved a great stimulus to further thinking not only about the individual child under discussion but about the related problems of record-taking techniques, the inter-relation of various kinds of data in the study of growth, and many other problems. These working sheets are presented here because of the value they have in suggesting a way of thinking about children.

At the close of this section a statement in Miss Johnson's own words explains the psychological point of view from which the records were taken.

## NOTES ON THE STUDY OF INDIVIDUAL CHILDREN IN A SCHOOL SITUATION

### A STUDY OF ONE CHILD'S IMMATURE RESPONSE TO THE NURSERY SCHOOL CURRICULUM

Myra A. (In attendance from 2 years, 0 months to 2 years, 8 months)

After children have been for some weeks in the Nursery School, the teachers are likely to give them an informal and generalized sort of ranking in various performances. We base our judgments upon standards of behavior at the different age levels and usually make them quite empirically. In other words, there are certain expectations that we hold regarding a child of eighteen months, of twenty-four months, of thirty-six months, expectations which we have gained through observing and recording the behavior of children of those ages operating in an environment which remains fairly stable.

In this report we have tried to analyze our impressions of Myra, going back to the records for a large part of the material which we present. We have not tried to make a full statement of the responses we expect from a child of her age, but have attempted, rather, to show typical immaturities in her behavior, and the unevenness of her development.

The outstanding difference between Myra and the usual nursery child lies more in the things to which she does not react, the situations to which she is oblivious, than in positive ways of behaving toward people or things.

A citation from the records of November 18 to 25 will show something of our state of mind about Myra after about one month in the Nursery School, age 25 months, 15 days.

We have been much puzzled about the significance of Myra's reactions and are suspending our judgment until we can get an array of her patterns.

She is retarded in her language—in vocabulary and in understanding. She seems not to expect to find meaning in language, so does not attend even when it is directed specifically to her. Her vocabulary is very limited, and she uses few well articulated syllables. Some of her sounds seem curiously unformed and almost animal-like.

On the other hand, her rhythmic phrases are tuneful and especially definite and "true," i.e. they follow convention in pitch and intervals, so that her incidental music can be readily verified.

She uses her body well, though her run is babyish, especially in the accessory movements of arms and hands. Her hands seem to us to be used with vague and indefinite motions. She patters in short steps, her arms and hands waving and bobbing with her body. There is no wavering in her locomotion. She gets over the ground with an automatic ease and precision which marks her as well beyond the three younger children, Alice, Richard, and Sara, all under two years old. She does more with her body than Larry, also, but I should say that was a matter of interest and busy-ness rather than of efficiency. (Larry is twenty-one months.)

She seems to have her quota of "motor understanding" and vigilance. Her muscles do her bidding in problems of leverage, for example. She takes on readily such patterns as sliding. Has learned to use the indoor and outdoor slide, and has not been noted as losing the pattern, once it was established.

Her obliviousness and immaturity show themselves in the social situation. She seemed at first not to notice adults or children. She took adult requirements without demur; adjusted completely, and seemingly with no feeling, to the nursery situation, but made no overt response to adults and children. Seemed not concerned with activities of children and only quite recently has been seen to watch them with real awareness in her gaze and posture. There must have been observations of their activities, for she has used quite a variety of toys and apparatus.

As repeated records show, she does not take directions, even when they are specifically addressed to her and when the remarks are reinforced by gesture.

We have raised various questions which it may be well to state here.

Is there a mental deficiency or retardation?

Can it be that vision or hearing is not normal?

Is the difficulty entirely in her environment? When we spoke to her mother about her failure to take directions, she said that Myra had never been given directions. That is surely unusual at two and suggests either a peculiar point of view or lack of understanding on the part of the parents.

Her response to the experience in the nursery school suggests that her inadequacies may be largely lack of opportunity, but that does not seem to us an entirely sufficient answer to our questions. We shall continue to study Myra's reactions with the help of the physician and a further history from her mother, and then we may have tests given her to see if they throw any light upon her mental and physical equipment.

## General physical condition

Physically Myra's body is well developed, and she has it under good control. She showed no reluctance in adjusting to the nursery environment, which now seems due, perhaps, to a lack of understanding or attention. She chose and used the expected variety of materials, and from the first has given us the feeling that she needed very little supervision in situations requiring muscular control.

Her gait is very peculiar. She thrusts her head out and down, sometimes walking in a slouching "ploughboy" manner.

We have commented many times upon an indecisive quality that she has, especially in the use of her hands. However, everything that one says about Myra must be qualified. She can tower blocks, and she feeds herself now with comparatively little spilling, so belying the charge of inadequate use of her hands; but she rarely points with a forefinger. The vagueness referred to will be mentioned again in the discussion of delayed and aborted reactions.

The school physician reports that the physical examination reveals nothing which could positively account for her retarded development. He questioned a sudden rise of temperature before she had a tonsillectomy several months ago, but that seems to have been due to an ear infection. The reflexes were normal: the Babinski was not positive; and the knee jerk, though hyperactive, was not unusually so.

*Visual peculiarities*

Another physical peculiarity about which we have raised a question is the appearance of her eyes and her method of using them. I am not now referring to her strabismus, which may or may not be significant. Citations from the records describe situations in which she has not responded as most children do to a visual stimulus.

> *October 22* (2;0)* Carries her head craned forward a little and bent down. Seems not to look up often.
>
> *November 26* (2;2) . . . led to toilet, hung on adult's hand, sagging body, head not held upright.
>
> *November 26* (2;2) During music. Some sort

* Here and in all following instances the figures within parentheses indicate the child's age on the day on which the record was taken, to be read, in this instance, two years, no months.

of posturing going on. Raised chin and let eye-
lids fall over eyes.

*December 20* (2;2) Watched visitor's feet as
she passed her from kitchen to hall. Did not look
up toward her face. (Was using link blocks on
floor.)

*January 30* (2;4) Looked up when light was
switched on in blockroom.

Tips head far back, bowing her back in and
half closing eyes, when she is asking adults for
something.

*February 27* (2;5) As she sits today, her eyes
have a particularly unfocused lackluster expression. Adult able to duplicate by deliberately
taking expression from her eyes and letting them
float up so that whites are visible underneath.

*April 30* (2;7) Myra the only one of group of
six, who did not grow excited and watch aeroplane. Adult made every effort to show it to her.
Same thing noticed last week, though on that
occasion her attention was not called to it by
adult.

*May 8* (2;7) Aeroplane heard overhead.
Mary, four feet from Myra, shouted "Dere's a
aer'p'ane." Myra made no move that suggested
that she heard it. Others all saw and expressed
excitement over it. Sound continued. When it
was dying down, she raised her head and seemed
to listen but did not raise eyes skyward at any
time. Sound gone. After a little she began to
talk to herself.

*May 9* (2;7) Entire group (six children) grew
excited, pointed and shouted as aeroplanes flew
noisily overhead. Myra only one of group to

remain apparently unmoved. She paid absolutely no attention and hung to trapeze with
knees flexed, feet off tiles, swinging.

*May 9* (2;7) Myra climbing on rope ladder of
tower gym. Mary returned and swung her as
zeppelin flew overhead. Mary soon joined excited group watching zeppelin, but Myra never
left ladder.

*May 27* (2;8) Adult lifted Myra in her arms
and tried her best to show her an aeroplane that
was shining silver in the sunlight and also making a good deal of noise. Myra seemed definitely
to resist the effort of adult to make her raise her
eyes to sky level. (All the other children were
making much of the aeroplane as usual.)

It seems almost as if Myra had a limited range of
vision, especially for distance and elevation. She has
been noted as looking up to the balcony of the indoor slide and responding to a call from a child there,
but for the most part the things that gain her attention are those that lie within a narrow field immediately about her. We have no note of her looking into
the sky, across to distant roofs, up to chimney pots,
or down into the school yards. The sun and clouds,
people or whirling ventilators on the roofs of houses
near and far, and children playing in the school yard,
are subjects of lively comment and interest with all
our children.

Whatever vision defect she may have, it does not
show the usual manifestations. She discriminates between block shapes; she sees and picks up small ob-

jects without fumbling. The things she disregards are other children, open doors, and distant views.

### Level of language responsiveness

Obliviousness to language has been an outstanding characteristic. Myra has made considerable progress in taking directions since her first months with us. Even in November, however, she was not always consistently inattentive. For instance, after uniformly ignoring all directions during the forenoon, she responded to an invitation to get milk after nap by going at once to the kitchen with an adult.

The outstanding difference between Myra and the others is a tendency to periods of vagueness during which her general tone is on a low level; inquiries and directions fail to catch her attention, she resorts to thumb sucking more frequently, and her expression seems unfocused.

A comment from the dietitian is found on May 9 (2;7).

> EB has observed that during Myra's periods of vagueness she eats more avidly and with less apparent awareness of her surroundings.

This observation was made rather late in the year and was not followed up. However, there appear early in the school year several descriptions of her eating habits: eagerness over food, cramming her mouth, and "animal-like gestures."

Examples follow of the kind of obliviousness she showed when given directions:

*November 26* (2;2) Adult: "Go and sit down and have banana." Directions repeated about three times with no effect, then she was led to seat.

*November 26* (2;2) Adult, washing Myra for dinner: "Give me your other hand, please. Give me your other hand, please. Give me your other hand, please. Myra, give me your other hand. Let me have your other hand." Myra laughed and made absolutely no move with hands. Seemed to be quite unaware of any connection between herself and the words.

*December 20* (2;2) . . . Willa working at her nail beside Myra. Willa laid her hammer down on table to use fingers on a nail. Myra picked it up with right hand, her own hammer in her left. Willa squawked and claimed it. Myra was asked several times, "Where is *your* hammer?" Seemed oblivious of her own hammer and kept reaching insistently for Willa's. Finally her own hammer was taken from her left hand and held out in front of her. She took it. . . . It seemed as if she had lost the hammer she held in left hand.

*January 6* (2;3) Myra took the direction to put hands on her stomach during weighing, although there was no observable facial expression to indicate that the direction had been comprehended or even heard. This is very typical of her.

*January 20* (2;3) Richard, Myra, Molly, and Willa at shelter table, all but Myra with hammers, nails, and blocks. (Children drive their nails into hollow blocks.) She had seemed twice to want a hammer but had ignored directions, carefully repeated, to "get a block, a big block," etc. and had settled down to watch the others. After a time, adult spoke to her by name. Myra did not stir a muscle. Adult repeated her name, then continued to repeat it, making every effort to use such emphasis as could not fail to attract her attention. The effort was so conspicuous that both Molly and Willa stopped their hammering and gazed long at Myra, who did not stir a muscle as she sat looking at Richard's work.

*March 4* (2;5) Myra does not respond by the faintest stir of muscle or change of breath to the direction "blow" or "blow your nose," when a handkerchief or piece of paper is held for the purpose.

### Delayed and aborted reactions

When she makes a response, it is unusual and peculiar. The delayed reaction is expected with children younger than Myra. The baby who says "Good-bye" after the guest has closed the door no longer surprises us. Myra also does this. She also frequently makes what we have called an aborted reaction. She gives one the impression that she is about to respond promptly and decisively, then the impulse seems not strong enough to carry her through to the indicated response.

In some cases her failure to respond seems to be an inattention to language, but in these cited below there seems to be an interruption to a process initiated by the child herself.

*January 27* (2;4) When Myra was told to get a chair at milk time, a blue chair was about a foot from table. She looked around room, walked to east shelves, started to push yellow chair, looked about again, and very definitely showed that she wanted lavender chair which she saw near chute. She pushed it very near table, then sat supinely in the blue chair which had been there from the beginning of her tour. She made no gesture to move chair to table where her cup of milk sat nor to move table to chair, nor did she respond in any way when adult told her to stand up.

One early record (see record, November 26, below) had shown her as being able to set her chair in satisfactory position at table.

*November 26* (2;2) Was told to place chair. Took it by back in both hands, raised it, and placed it directly at table, pushing it well under. Pulled it out a bit and slid in.

*April 4* (2;6) Was asked where her towel was. Arms and hands went out as if she were about to point, then muscles slackened and arms dropped at sides.

*April 14* (2;6) Myra, bothering Larry with his wagonload of pebbles in the pit, was asked if she would like to play in the sand. Said, "Aw ri'," turned over to her hands instantly and rose. Went to large packing box, in some way got herself into it and began to collect pans (a logical preparation for sand play). Was seen apparently trying unsuccessfully to get out. Adult tried to help; Myra resisted and settled on green board laid from slat to slat to arrange her pans. A little later she squawked as she tried to get out between slats, was helped over top, seized some pans from adult's hand to add to her own four, took all to slide steps, climbed, threw all the pans down the chute with a clatter, and slid after them head first on stomach. Repeated, laughing aloud at the clatter. Was seen to be wet, so was taken, resisting with squawks, to be changed.

The sand boxes had been opened just before adult suggested them to Myra, and the four other children had hurried to them at once. Myra did not cast a glance toward them at any time. She has a surprising power of seeming oblivious to things that the other children react to at once.

It seems as if in a situation which demands steps to be taken preliminary to a desired end, Myra is swamped by the detail and loses her purpose before she gets to it.

Somewhat similar to the aborted reactions are what we have noted as delayed responses, those coming after a circuitous ramble. Sometimes her immediate response promises to be appropriate, that is, she seems about to take the suggestion; sometimes she seems oblivious to it but ends by following it.

*February* 27 (2;5) Was told to find her bed. Off first toward west room, then by a very circuitous route to north room (where her bed was).

*May 8* (2;7) . . . tried to take a shovel from Larry. It was returned to him, and she was told to go to the shelter and get a shovel. She set off toward block stacks (north) as though with no intent to take the suggestion, circled around to pit, over curb in the vicinity of the slide, whence she finally emerged with a sink shovel.

*May 8* (2;7) . . . came to recorder with whom Molly had left her hat and took it. Was told to "take it to Harriet." Circled around and finally ended up by giving it to HS at the far side of the room.

Many of the stimuli to which children react fail to get Myra's attention. All the younger children of eighteen to twenty-eight months roughly tend to drift, singly or en masse, toward any door which is left open. Myra has never been noted as making this tropistic response.

One outstanding example of this was given in a full-day record taken on December 20. Myra was the first child awake in the afternoon. The City and Country School children were singing Christmas carols in the gymnasium, the door of which was open. As Myra went into the play room, an adult opened the nursery door to the hall and propped it back with a keg. Myra looked at the keg but gave no sign of hearing music or of seeing children. She played with interlocking blocks at the toy closet, which is near the door. Once the adult tried to call her attention to the music, asking "Do you hear any music, Myra?" She gave no sign of hearing either the question or the music. We felt sure that any other child in the group would have been so aware of what was going on outside that he would have attempted an investigation.

A classic game with babies is asking them to point out their eyes, noses, mouths, and such features. Her mother says Myra answered all these questions before she was two. However, the records below give characteristic responses of Myra to these questions, at the same time showing that a learning process is going on.

> *November 26* (2;2) While dressing Myra after her nap, adult tested her on usual baby tricks: "Where is your nose?—mouth?" Myra interested only in getting off the table. Showed no sign of understanding. Smiled and stretched arms out toward adult, but made no response, and when LW tried the game of finding arms, nose, etc. there was also no response.
>
> *January 30* (2;4) Was asked questions about nose, ear, hat. Only response a broad smile and a syllable or so. Not the slightest suggestion that words of adult had meaning for her.
>
> *January 30* (2;4) No sort of response to various personal questions re: nose, John, Millie.
>
> *February 27* (2;5) Questions regarding nose, eyes, mouth, hand, foot, tried by LW. At "nose," Myra looked over edge of dressing table. No response for eyes or other members. Then Myra raised thumb toward face in such a position that we thought she was going to suck it. Instead she gradually brought it up to nose. Matter of identifying features not pressed.

*March 4* (2;5) Myra was asked, "Where is your nose?" She smiled a little in her undirected way, then flung out right arm and swung hand in toward her but did not approach her nose. It seemed like an aborted response to the question, but what aborted it is difficult to say. Myra has always shown many either delayed or incomplete responses.

*April 30* (2;7) Myra, seated on chamber with two hands full of beads brought from home, was asked where her nose was. She smiled after just an instant's pause, raised her left hand, and, with forefinger extended, touched her lips.

*May 1* (2;7) Myra touched adult's hair. Was asked what it was, then given the word. Adult then asked, "Where is your hair? Where is Myra's hair?" With hand somewhat wavering and slow, Myra finally touched her own hair, smiling. Also touched her nose when asked where it was. First time we have ever succeeded in getting her to do this as a direct response to the question.

## Range of social awareness

That Myra's obliviousness extends to persons and to the social environment is shown in the records. It is obvious that a child who has little language at her command will be less mature in her social relationships with children than one who has language facility. An early record, made in October (2;0), shortly after her arrival, states:

Here and there around room, in and out

among children, but without appearing to attend to them. She seems to watch others less than any child I recall.

Again on May 8 (2;7):

> Arriving on roof: all other children happened to be in a loose grouping near swings, but she threw no glance in their direction.
>
> In sand box. Played independently; no communication with other children.

However, there was a process of orientation going on which the records reveal.

> *March 3* (2;5) Myra has little close contact with other children yet, but seems more aware of the social possibilities in adults than she used to be. She meets one's eyes more directly and with a genuine smile at dressing time, for instance. Occasionally she is seen gazing at an adult, less frequently at a child, with an air of scrutiny as though she were learning something about people from her long look. Once this week she seated herself with cubes on the floor near an adult who sat at adult table. The adult rose after a time, went into bathroom where another child was being dressed, and talked for a few moments. Myra followed soon, took her by the hand and led her back, dropping her at the chair she had been sitting in; and when adult seated herself again, Myra dropped to the floor and continued to build.
>
> *March 10* (2;5) Myra seems to be arriving at the early social stage of experimenting with

human beings. Her method is not very agreeable but is probably necessary and valuable for her at this point. She does such things as standing very near another child and if pushed away, returns at once just as near, watching the other's face as she does it. Once she stood at the foot of Sara's bed and when Sara protested, "Dat's my bed!" she jerked up the crepe cover; Sara straightened it down, and Myra jerked it up again, watching her face with a faint smile. Did this repeatedly until adult intervened. She also makes gestures of attack though I have never seen her quite hit anyone, I think. Was building once on chest in block room when Richard came to within about four feet of her. She immediately shouted "No! No!" and hurried toward him, beating up and down with both arms. Adult spoke quickly, and she did not hit him.

*May 8* (2;7) Recorder called her by name. Myra turned toward her almost at once. Was told to push down her bloomers and sit on a chamber. She smiled, eyes meeting adult's with one of her looks, not by any means customary, of perfect intelligence and awareness, pushed down her bloomers with both hands, went to corner and dragged out large blue chamber, drew it near recorder's feet, and sat down on it. Smiled at recorder as she did this.

During the last month (2;7—2;8), there have been various group activities in which she has joined.

Others bouncing on planks. She hurried over and sat in the row. This is one of the few kinds of group play that she joins readily now with obvious enjoyment. Smiled and vocalized while two older children alternately bounced her and two younger ones.

There follows an instance of her lack of concern with what is done to her:

> Mary, bouncing behind her, bent over her and finally bowed her flat, with head between her feet. Not a sound came from Myra, not even a look of distress as she rose from her prostration.
>
> Began to sprinkle sand out on tiles. Was lifted into sand box by adult and made no sound of objection. She pays surprisingly little attention to what is done to her.

She is noted on several occasions as making no response in kind to attacks.

> Sara kicked at her. Myra gave inarticulate outcries but did not move away or retaliate.

There were several baby games that she played with one or the other of the younger children.

> Richard, two years old, carried two stools from shelter, placed them evenly with long sides against pebble curb. As soon as he sat upon one, scuffing feet back and forth on tiles, Myra sat upon the other and scuffed her feet. They smiled at each other.
>
> Myra played a game with Richard in new sand box in which she repeatedly poured a little sand on the cover and he promptly brushed it

away. They did this probably twelve or more times in succession, Myra smiling widely, Richard less exuberantly but carrying his part steadily.

These were high spots in Myra's awareness of her mates.

## Absence of dramatic play

Dramatic reproduction of past experiences is an outstanding characteristic of small children. It is so universal that it is the keynote of our curriculum planning, and our choice of equipment is largely based upon their need of raw materials to help them make vivid their dramatization. The earliest form of dramatic reproduction has to do with feeding. A child under two often pretends to eat, either merely by motions or with pebbles which he actually puts in his mouth. The intricacies of dramatization we do not expect to find imitated or initiated under two years, but from then on such intimate experiences as going to bed, taking baths, having hair washed and shoes shined, are reproduced by practically all children in greater or less detail. There are no notes in our records of Myra of any sort of dramatization, and none of us has any memory of even a suspicion that implicit or overt rehearsal was going on.

## Growing language facility

During the last two months, (2;6—2;8), her actual vocabulary has increased, and, what is still more significant, she has begun asking "Hussat?" or "Whussat?" of various things and persons. This means that a language interest has been aroused, though she has rarely repeated the word that was given her.

She has a peculiarity in her pronunciation of the initial letter *s*. She makes a curious thickened gutteral sound, apparently not bringing her teeth together to give it the hissing quality.

When she came to us, she had a very limited number of words, "bye, bye," "ni', ni'," "no," and "go 'way." These she applied to any situation, relevant or otherwise. She still does this in a measure, though we realize that what sounds irrelevant to us may be relevant to her. The following examples are taken from her May record, (2;7—2;8):

> Murmured "bye bye" twice softly as she squatted in sand box, brushing sand into one hand with the other.

This remark sounds inappropriate but may have had significance to her.

> Was seated with crayons. Talked to herself. "No! No! No, Myra! No, Myra. Aw right. No, Myra."

She has never, to our knowledge, spoken of herself by name, but uses this term "No, Myra" as a general negative.

> Myra had been dragging her coat about on the floor, and adult had taken it from her to put into her basket. Thereupon she sauntered about desultorily, thumb in mouth, eyes dull and rolled

slightly upward. Adult said, "Don't you want to go and build with some blocks?" Myra turned away, saying mildly, "No, Myra."

The record of April 21 to 28 (2;7) gives this list of words:

> Myra is gradually adding to her vocabulary. "pin," "ussat" (What's that?), "doh" (door), "aw ri'" (all right), "soap," "toat" (coat), "djump" (jump), "Mee-e" (Millie).

She has added several others since then.

A note during the week of April 28 (2;7) is as follows:

> Along with her gradually growing vocabulary of real words, Myra continues at intervals to utter sharp, inarticulate, animal-like yelps. They sound so much like the squawks of the injured party in some familiar nursery disagreement over materials, that frequently an adult hurries to the scene only to find Myra sitting peacefully with pans and covers or roaming around the room serenely.
>
> She continues also from time to time to say, "No, Myra; no, Myra" on occasions when she might logically be expected to be saying, "No, Sandy," or "No, Larry." She uses no names for nursery adults except EB—"Mee-e" (heard only once; did not become established). Mary is the only child's name which we have been able to identify.

*May 8* (2;7) She has lately acquired Sara's

name (heard only once, but then appropriately).

We are not sure where the expression, "No, Myra,"
arose. The older children have said it to her when
she interfered with their work, and one child is
recorded as exhorting her thus about sucking her
thumb. Myra has applied it as a unit word to other
children and to inanimate objects.

She has several phrases which she treats as words.

> "Un-a-ge-dow" (want to get down)
> "Un-a-ge-dop" (want to get up)
> "Un-go" (want to go)
> "Un-bi" (want bib)
> "Un-bok" (want box)
> "Un-a-moh" (want more)

## Responsibility for routines

The nursery program provides first of all for children to gain independence in their play activities, so
that they will find opportunity for elaborated and
experimental use of the play materials. We regard
self-help in practical matters as one of many means
toward attaining independence, but not as an end in
education. Opportunities are given for children to
gain facility in the care of their own persons and an
understanding of the program and the day's routine.

Myra's interest in dressing seemed to be progres-
sing well at the end of the year.

> *February 21* (2;4) . . . makes weak gestures
> to put arms through arm holes of clothing but

seems very vague and not aware that any co-operation is expected of her.

*March 31* (2;6) When told to put panties on, Myra held upper edge of them against low bathroom table and raised one foot, then the other, to table edge in effort to put them into opening.

*May 8* (2;7) . . . rose from chamber of her own accord, looked at adult with a smile as though expecting comment; as none was forthcoming, she pulled up her bloomers by the sides.

Made an excellent attempt at putting on left stocking, drawing knee up and raising foot from table. Put both shoes on alone (low, single-strap pumps).

. . . sat giving some attention to the process of getting the bloomers off over her feet. Was told to take off shoes and socks (each of four garments told separately) and took direction each time. Adult said, "Now your shirt." Myra promptly looked down in front of her where shirt buttons might be expected to be found. . . . Was helped. . . .

Other records show that she sought her table after being washed, that she rose from table or toilet of her own accord, and that she sometimes carried her cup to the serving table after eating.

Her toilet habits suffered a lapse during the winter, coincident, we judged, with an emotional home situation. In February there were several instances of involuntary urination, and in March the following note was made:

*March 3* (2;5) After a period of occasionally leading an adult to the bathroom and
pulling out a chamber, an obvious request to be
unbuttoned, Myra has dropped back to depending entirely upon adults. Twice this week she
has sat with dolls and covers on the floor and has
wet thoroughly, with so little outward concern
that only the flood of water coming out around
her has given her away.

She has fed herself from the beginning, and her
technique has steadily improved. She does a very inadequate job at washing her hands, but only the old-
est of our children can be credited with anything
approaching a real technique. She finds her way up
the three flights of stairs to the nursery floor alone.
This is a privilege granted to the chosen few who are
almost or quite three years old.

*Play activities*

Myra is usually a busy person. She has used a great
variety of material; has acquired certain skills, like
bouncing on a spring board, riding a kiddy kar, setting and driving nails, and using a swing.

We have records of her making an adequate reaction to such problem situations as interlocking blocks
and freeing a wagon wheel which was caught on an
obstruction, but she does not seem to seek materials
which present such problems.

The blocks have attracted her from the first, and
she has done some excellent balancing stunts in building towers, which show that her hands work more

deftly and accurately than their somewhat vague and wavering appearance suggests. Her buildings however are uncomplicated and show little distinction except for their problems in balance.

In March she accomplished bridging, which seems to be very difficult for the young. We have watched her in the process and have seen her set two blocks on end, get another of the same length, and immediately move the first two nearer to each other before attempting to put the third across the space.

During the last month of the school year (2;7 to 2;8), her interest in blocks seemed to lapse. For three weeks there was no mention of block building in the records.

A few examples of her block structures earlier in the year follow:

> *January 30* (2;4) Four posts and two half-units given her. Said "bwock," then "b'ock." Built as sketched, with no hesitation. Did not knock it down. Structure fell when she moved.

> When two more half-units were given her, she laid an irregular flooring, blocks not fitted together at all.

*February 3* (2;4) Myra lined seven cubes along end of cube box, a stunt that needs some care in balancing, as the edge is narrower than the cubes.

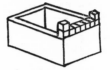

Later she achieved a tower seven cubes high above a line of four on end of box. Eighth cube broke the tower. Chanted "Aw gone" from time to time in a soft sweet voice. She did this, I think, always when a cube fell and had to be placed again, a thing which happened frequently.

*March 3* (2;5) Once she had two posts upright at an appropriate distance apart for bridging with another. Tried to lay one across them, but in the process knocked over the first-placed one. Set it up, then balanced one post on top of only one of the uprights. Did not achieve a bridge unit while watched. (See record and illustration, April 16.)

*March 19* (2;5) Myra made these arrangements and others of posts. Her hands usually look vague and fluttering as she works, but she gets surprisingly even results.

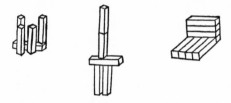

*April 16* (2;6) Myra . . . set down two units on end, more or less parallel, got another unit, laid it with left hand crosswise on the left-hand unit (as she faced them), holding it thus while with right hand she moved right-hand unit in toward left-hand one until the cross-piece could reach it. Stood another unit briefly at the doorway, then took bridge apart and, after some manipulations, built another by the same method. Added to this. Details not taken, but she had it two blocks high for a time.

*April 21* (2;6) Myra built this almost at once upon arrival:

She has not yet shown the tendency to elaborate her simple motor patterns or her block building designs as children often do at her age. On the other hand, she has developed the usual interest in practicing motor performances like stepping down from the curb or from the piece of apparatus known as three-steps; in jumping flatfooted; and, as before noted, in asking the names of things.

We have made only brief mention of Myra's "music." We have many pages of phrases sung by the children, some of them approximate only, but many verified. Early in the year the comment was made that Myra's singing voice was sweet, clear, and unusually true. We have not included these records.

———

As I read over these notes of Myra's, I fear that they fail to give a picture of her, after all; and especially that they do not adequately show her progress.

She seems to us to have become during the year a much more definite personality than she was, more aware of her own place in the group and of other persons, adults and children, as an actual part of the environment. We are puzzled and disturbed by these periods when her newly acquired definiteness seems to subside. It seems almost like a withdrawal from contact with the demands of people, a suspension of her awareness and interest in humankind about her. She is less likely to cease her activities with materials; but sometimes she seems dull-eyed and desultory and resorts to thumbsucking, covering the left ear with the left hand at the same time. Adults have commented that many other children may occasionally seem impervious to adult language, but there is no other child through whose outer crust of obliviousness it is so difficult to break.

Because of the progress that she has made during the past eight months, we have the hope that if she has time enough, in an environment in which she feels secure and which challenges her, though not too insistently, to social and mental participation, Myra will more and more nearly approach the standards for her age, and will be able to function up to her full capacity.

## A DEVELOPMENTAL COMPARISON OF TWO CHILDREN
### OF THE SAME AGE

Frances J. (In attendance from 1 year, 8 months to
  2 years, 4 months)
Greta M. (In attendance from 1 year, 2 months to
  2 years, 4 months)*

The differences in the behavior of the two children under discussion may be due to differences in
inherited structure or in environment or in physical
condition, and are probably due to all three. In
studying the records, I have taken certain large headings and have placed side by side the recorded observations. Under these headings I have summarized
the way in which the children compare with each
other.

> *Postural Activities.* Here I have included their
> methods of handling their bodies and adjusting
> to demands made upon them by situations en-
> countered.
> *Language Activities.* I have tried to show on
> the one hand the use the two children have
> made of their vocal apparatus, and on the other
> hand their sensitivity to auditory stimuli; and,
> further, how their own speech activities serve
> them.

* In making this study, Miss Johnson used only those records of Greta which were taken from 1 year, 8 months to
2 years, 2 months, thus making a parallel set of records with
those available on Frances. This material was used for a report to staff made during the month of March two months
previous to the close of the school year.

*Rhythmic Activities.* Their responses during music are allied to the activity of the speech mechanisms, but the records seem to show interesting differentiations here.

*Social Activities.* There was a considerable difference in the ways in which the two children reacted to and made use of the social situation.

*Immaturities.* Both children showed uneven development. I have attempted to get from the records a picture of each child's "blind spots."

Greta entered the nursery school last year, Frances the first day of school this fall. They made their initial adjustments with no difficulty.

Frances is a closely knit, well rounded little person. Her face presents no lines or angles but is curved. Her hands are plump and firm. She has a normal quota of teeth.

Greta is quite a different type. Her body is beautifully modelled but is built on a larger bony frame, I should judge. We have compared her to a character doll. Her facial expression changes more than Frances's whose range of facial expression is much more limited and much less under her own control. Greta puts on expressions of wonder, amazement, question, etc. She also makes many motions with her hands, fingers, and wrists. Her tongue is less active now than earlier, but it is still in evidence as a useful member. Her dentition is much delayed, and she has many physical difficulties when teeth are erupting. She occasionally has intestinal upsets, with appetite much lessened, and lately had two long grippy colds which seemed to be caused by teething. Her resistance, apparently, was lowered, so that she was more susceptible.

## Postural activities

An early record, of October 4, gives the first walking habits of the two children and the impressions of the staff in regard to them.

> *October 4* (1;8) Frances, twenty months, fourteen days; rather small head, prominent frontal bosses, very sturdy legs. Ankles looked very slightly inverted; but her laced shoes were high, and it was not possible to say definitely. She was active, trotting but not running the first day. Laid two brooms down on the floor and stepped over the handles. A visible effort in her performance.
>
> Goes up over sills from shelter to roof with much effort. Put flat of hand against door jamb and very deliberately balanced herself on one foot and drew up the other. A platform over a wet place on the roof had been placed in front of door but not flush against sill. Space not over three inches wide; but she hesitated, tipped forward on her toes, and withdrew back into the shelter. Stepped down without hesitation when platform was pulled away. She shows this consciousness of spaces consistently.
>
> While using wheelbarrow, she stepped down into the drain depression, a square hollow place. Moaned, but made no effort to get out on her own power.

Down on hands and feet to go over threshold between playroom and extension.

Called nurse when she wished to get off curb of pebble pit. Was assured that she could get down alone. Put one foot tentatively on curb, standing. Withdrew. Later, when left alone, she dropped to hands and knees, thrust one foot over and down on to tiles, then turned and backed down.

Climbed to top of three-steps as they stood against south wall. Was observed stepping cautiously along top step, one hand on wall, saying, "Come down, come down." Held out hand to adult for help. As she made no attempt to get down alone, adult finally took her hand, and she walked down forwards.

Frances walks with short quick steps, her hands held in front of her, elbows flexed, wrists relaxed. They seem to help her keep her balance. If she makes a misstep, one or both arms go up in the air. Forefingers extend as hands go up. No babyish waddle in her gait, though it is not mature: a jerk in trunk, and very short steps. She bends over, taking the bear position, a good deal. Was observed to follow it by extending one leg out behind, tip of toe touching floor. Walks with head slightly forward, arms flexed at elbows, fingers spread, appearance of walking on heels.

*October 8* (1;9) Her method of taking sills and platform has quite changed. Put left hand against jamb. Did not raise feet high, but did walk across and, with no support, off platform, a short two inches high.

Note has been made of her getting stalled in

the pebble drain. As she was playing with a ball, it rolled into the drain. She looked at it, then waved her hand and said, "Way, way." Greta also saw it and squatted some distance from it, reached out, and moved four fingers over the rough surface of the ball, making movements toward her till she rolled the ball out.

*October 22* (1;9)  Going over curb of pebble pit from the tiles, she planted her hands over in the pebbles, put her right knee on the curb, slung her left foot, with knee straight, around in a wide circle into the pebbles, and, bracing on hands, rose from knees to standing position. Done with almost no hesitation and with good speed.

Unable to get off three-steps which were against the wall under window in pebbles. Began to tread back and forth on the top step, whimpering "Uh uh uh." Several times she faced the window in proper position for backing down, but got no farther. She thrust one leg down from the top step; once from the side, bracing against the wall, but pulled it up again. Was disturbed, even after adult had helped her down to lowest step. Repeated performance of whimpering and treading up and down. When one foot was actually placed in the pebbles, she thrust the other down, too.

Climbed by the three-steps to top of small packing case but could not get back down the steps and was disturbed. This time after her feet were placed in position, she descended.

In rising, she puts hands on ground, then backs

them up almost to her toes to get the required push, then stands.

*October 26* (1;9)  Climbed three-steps and got down by herself.

*November 1* (1;9)  Both Greta and Frances cross shelter sill occasionally without steadying themselves by jamb. Frances walked about skylight seat three times, taking corners easily, then crept along one side. Slid off on stomach.

*November 8* (1;10)  Seesaw board laid across sawhorse. Adult held Frances's hand and let her walk up once. When the tip came she crouched and stiffened, registering alarm. Was reluctant about proceeding further along plank. Walked down seesaw after it was lowered.

With broom in right hand, Frances crossed sill without touching door jamb.

To summarize briefly: Frances showed marked hesitation and insecurity in her posture. In walking, she held arms flexed at the elbows, forearms out, hands flapping as if she needed a balancing pole. She hesitated in going over obstacles and showed an equal reluctance in getting up on the end of a board five inches above the ground. When she got her feet in a square depression holding the drain, she was entirely caught, and made no effort to get out. Later, when her ball went in, she did not venture near enough to reach it.

Turning to Greta, it should be mentioned that she was slow in establishing locomotion of any kind, but her use of her body was energetic during the last month of last year. Records of the current year read as follows:

*October 4* (1;8) Greta has the figure of a little girl rather than of a baby. Is taller and heavier than she was last spring. Her walking pattern is well developed, she stands straight, is steady on her feet, and negotiates sills easily. Her arm-shoulder girdle is very strong. Accounts are given of her lifting wheelbarrows and trailer. She is responsive to all advances, children's or adults', and seems altogether a fine, husky, well coordinated child. Very seldom ruffled by circumstances.

Greta trots about, with no jerk in her upper body as she steps. She is sure-footed and rarely falls. Elaborates her walking pattern with a sort of slow heavy galloping step, and on Friday did a real dance, jigging from foot to foot sideways in quick rhythm. Arms hang loose as she runs.

Greta is cultivating a caper. As she is heavy and rather flat-footed in her gait, it is not a tripping caper. She is experimenting with various steps. She sways back and forth from one foot to the other, or runs, thrusting right foot forward with an emphasized stamp. Body sways forward with her leg. Very rhythmic.

*October 21* (1;9) Her feet turn out and she tips from side to side as she walks. Uses legs freely, bends at knees, etc.

Pebble curb performance: stood some distance from curb, hands on curb; and with a wide spread, thrust right leg over curb and on to pebbles, pushed against platform, and then drew left leg up (body well over curb) and on to pebbles.

Crossed sill, one hand against door jamb, then stepped up. Shuffled across platform without lifting feet, then stepped down from platform to tiles, without support and with no apparent effort or awareness of the step as a difficulty. Later was able to step up on sill without help of pressure against door frame.

Walked up three-steps, hands on step, then knee up, then foot. Turned at top and seated self on window ledge. Descended by herself; stuck feet out straight so that they escaped edge of stair below, then bumped down on buttocks. Later went down again by this method, then tried to step down but sat down abruptly. Rose, tripped on edge of platform, and went down on hands and knees.

To get up on the end of a board hardly more than an inch high, she went down on hands and knees. Hands placed like a frog, she drew legs up alternately following hands, elbows flexed. Moved about sideways, pushed knees near the edge, felt for tiles, and then rose to feet. (She had evidently crawled up on higher part of board.) Gave a chuckling sort of escape of breath as she achieved it.

Turned and rose by a method almost exactly like hers of last year. Revolved, drawing up one knee, pulled other foot up beside it as slowly as reduced-speed motion picture, and thus got on knees, gradually bringing hands up near knees, then rose to feet.

Frances's outstanding ability was her method on stairs. She attacked them at once, creeping, and walked up and down without adult's hand fairly early. Stairs have been one of her home activities. However, as recorded, she was completely treed on the three-steps while Greta bumped down them, sitting. Her able performance on stairs was not applied to the steps at first. Three-steps have no rail.

Greta was completely stumped by the stairs and was reluctant in setting up her pattern. By October 21 (1;9) she "walked" up, her hands held by two adults. In this case, however, she did nothing but hang on the adults' hands and make her legs go from stair to stair, bearing no weight on them. On November 19 (1;10) Greta is recorded as creeping up till asked to walk, when she showed her usual tendency: as she goes up or down she takes the spindle near her, and so fails to get the assistance from it that is possible. In going up, she leaves her hand on a lower spindle, so that the tendency is to pull her back. In going down, she does not reach forward to a spindle near the lower step but leaves her hand on an upper one and is pulled back. Furthermore, Greta shuffles forward on each step, instead of thrusting leg forward and down at once.

On February 8 (2;0) it is recorded that she held lightly to spindles or top rail and that she took several steps down, unsupported; also that she stepped off the end of a plank set on the curb about five and a half inches above pebbles.

Frances mounts a kiddy kar normally, though with

effort. She was later in experimenting with kars than Greta, and does not use them much. There are very few records throughout the year so far. She has not yet achieved a good dismounting position.

A record of December 21 shows her characteristic procedure:

> *December 21* (1;11) Frances chose one of the largest kars. "Kaw." "Get on." Left hand on seat, right hand on handlebars (standing on right side of kar). "Get on. I want to get on." Went around to left side of kar. Left hand on bar, right on seat, she lifted and carried it a few steps. "Looka da kaw. Nice kaw. Here's the kaw. Wite dere. Look dat. He's nanna kaw." Right hand on seat, left on handle bars, she put right knee on seat: "Put sor foot up." Leaned over kar, hands in above position.
>
> Straightened and lifted again. Around to right side of kar. Has worked her way by this time to center table. She rested her right elbow on table, slowly lifted left leg and put it over kar, seated self and rode off slowly and laboriously, pushing with both feet together or using very tiny steps, one foot after the other. Said, "Way up in the air," as she came to sill. Stood astride kar and lifted front wheel twice, but not quite far enough to get it on the sill. "Wide over, ah can wide over." After saying this many times she tried a third time and made it. Much conversation about "Wide over." As back wheels stuck, adult encouraged her to go on. She poised, both feet on sill, front wheel out on tiles, back wheels half rolled up against sill, and looked back over

her shoulder at the back wheels. "Go on, Frances," spoken twice by adult. Patty gave her a push which sent kar over.

*March 1* (2;1)  Was observed drawing kar up to table so that she could get support for dismounting.

Greta's kar pattern is shown in the following records:

*October 4* (1;8)  Greta seated herself sidewise on a kar seat, doubled up left knee and worked her leg over across seat, in front of her and just back of handle bars. Dismounted by same method. Later tried to walk on from rear, astride. Rolled kar back and forth; did not, apparently, actually propel herself about on it.

*February 8* (2;0)  Held on by handle bars; and slowly and with evident effort at control, she lifted one foot to put it over; tipped about in attempt to get balance; but made it. Proceeded by her old method of digging her heels in.

This process has been described several times in the records. She seems to press with her body against the handlebars and, lifting both feet together, to thrust her heels down on the tiles and then push kar forward. One record says she achieved about three feet in a minute, jerking her body back and forth. Apparently she got better leverage when she sat far forward on the neck of the kar.

Frances adjusts to missteps or to sudden shifts of balance by flutterings throughout her body, arms flying up and fingers spread. The postures she assumes in preparation for an activity—a squat or a bend—are not stable.

*January 3* (1;11)  In laying doll covers out on the floor, she spread feet widely but with a base not stable enough to support her. Tipped forward toward toes and bent back on heels to recover. She had to shift and change as arm swing threw her off balance. Was compared with Tracy, whose squat holds him firmly; he can swing arms and rotate trunk without disturbing his position.

*February 1* (2;0)  To lay cubes, she sometimes tipped forward from heels to toes, bending only from hips. Squatted to gather them up. Lost balance and had to catch herself on her hands.

On March 1 (2;1) I tried to keep the two children in mind in observing Frances. There seems to be something almost spastic in Frances's movements. She takes and maintains a marked rigidity, whereas Greta, in spite of her occasional grotesque and awkward poses, gives one the feeling of a fluidity in movements and a general plasticity.

Greta makes her avoiding reactions less now, but occasionally a rapid motion near her will cause her to blink and dodge.

*February 28* (2;1)  Greta ran toward the inclined planks (ends raised on a pile of five yardblocks), when Patty and Charles suddenly came speeding down the incline on kars. She stopped so suddenly as almost to tip over; threw left arm up, almost across her face, and right arm out at side. Repeated each time a kar came down.

Early in the year in going down the slide, after she let herself slip she would tip over on her back, legs and arms flying out, legs spread.

As she stepped down off the platform, she "jigged" off, a side-to-side swaying, arms flying out.

On a certain occasion she wished to be swung. As the adult approached, she began to do a general full-body stirring, her face breaking into a smile. She did the same when she was given a cracker: an anticipatory flutter.

As a contrast to the avoiding reactions of Greta, it is interesting to note what is said of her ability to recover balance, her apparent muscle sense.

> *November 15* (1;10) On the seesaw she sat astride; has a natural sense for motion. Did not hold on; and with automatic precision, tipped body forward or back as board tipped up or down.
>
> Frances, on the seesaw, sat first with feet out on board, then astride, bending over and holding plank with both hands.

When the seesaw board was laid across a horse with its end on the tiles, and the children walked up and down it, taking the tip as their weight went beyond the center, Greta walked down and kept her balance. She was not slow or cautious. Frances gave every evidence of agitation and alarm when the board tipped down, showing that she had no expectation of what was going to happen. A short time later the following record occurs:

> *December 13* (1;11) Planks were set with one end of each on tiles, other ends meeting on three yard-blocks. Frances called it a seesaw and seated herself upon it. When urged to walk, she stepped cautiously from one to the other board, as if she expected a tip. Persisted in this mistake, repeatedly saying, "go" and "seesaw" and seating herself astride it. About eight minutes later she walked up one and down the other five times in succession.

Turning again to Greta, the poor economy shown in her stair climbing is also apparent in her plank bouncing and in her efforts at jumping. Adults have made valiant efforts to locate the muscular impulse of Greta's jump. In a square-footed jump off the floor it seemed to come from her waist muscles; that is, the lower trunk, not abdomen. In her bouncing there has been a painful period of experimenting when she has seemed to resort to general jerks of the trunk, failing signally to get into the rhythm. Tracy, in contrast, knows how to get the planks in motion by a bounce of his entire body, with motive power furnished by his legs, and how to keep it going by a series of very gentle straightenings and squats.

Greta is recorded in the week of March 3 (2;1) as having made a big advance in keeping her balance when older children are bouncing and in initiating the bounce herself. She is developing a smoother,

more continuous motion up into her trunk, from
bent knees, and down again.

*Language activities*

The citation about kiddy kars gave an indication
of the place of language activity in Frances's life. On
the first day the following comment was made:

> *October 4* (1;8) Vocalizes a great deal in a
> soft sweet voice. Murmurs as she plays about.
> Her inflections indicate that she is making sen-
> tences. We get few of her words unless she says
> something concerning the immediate situation.
> Repeats words after her family at home, and
> remembers them. Events prove that she does the
> same in the nursery. Her sentence structure is
> fairly complete. "I found dis." "Whadda nice
> book." (Everything is "nice.")

Once begun, language seems to take her along so
that her words flow beyond her awareness of their
meaning. Often this is evidently a recall of words she
has heard. "Taxicab waiting for you to go to school,"
said Frances when adult called to her that the taxicab
had come. Her remarks regarding the car sounded
like echoes of what had been said to her. Some of her
mistakes are due to obstructed breath, some to her
substituting the use of an object for its name: "Wan'
poun'," (hammer); "Wan' nap," (doll's bed);
"Dassa turn," (doll's joints).

The last week in October (1;9) Frances remembered "Down for music." Now she is likely to ask
for music at approximately the right hour. She echoes

almost every call made by adults and sings changes on it. An adult said, "Let's put this on." "Pood dis on, pood dis on," she chanted a dozen times or more. In October she is noted as employing many syllables as well as words and varying her tones. Repeated the syllables "Dah-bah" given her by adult as follows: on G, on C, on B, on C, on G, on C. Consonant sounds are varied. She swings into rhythm often.

*November 18* (1;10) Adult inquired, "Shall we get a ball?" Frances: "S'all we, s'all we, s'all we get a ball?" holding the conclusion of the sentence in mind without getting lost.

*December 13* (1;11) "Mam mam mam ma
　　　　　　　　Gum gum gum
　　　　　　　　Gum-a gum-a gum-a"
　　　　　　　"Get up, way up, go," sliding a block down.

*January 4* (1;11) "Toopsy—toopsy—too," a greeting to soup.

*February 1* (2;0) "Uk a la
　　　　　　Uk a la
　　　　　　Here a come
　　　　　　Here a come
　　　　　　Oh am am," she chanted as she wheeled a barrow.

*February 14* (2;1) Was handling a small shovel and a few pebbles. Said "Shov-oo" twenty-two times, mostly in the middle register, but occasionally rising. Repeated "stone" seven times; "Put it in," ten times.

*March 1* (2;1) Frances talks to herself incessantly, and her language seems to carry her along to more language. Dora and Ann used to carry on a sort of frenzied activity which we discouraged, but we felt that it was necessary to explain why we did not consider it legitimate or advantageous. I feel that Frances's language is sometimes a similar exercise of laryngeal muscles. But of course it is more, because the sound of a word or an expression sets off other words, not other postural activities.

Sat in swing, saying "I'm swinging, n'at funny," repeating this phrase at least eight times. Then "N'at funny swing," three times. "Now ha' more. Nudder swing. Nudder swing for daddy. Nudder swing for mommie. 'N one for you. 'N one for Paul. 'N one for grammie." (This is a recall of the "long, long drink for mother" song). "An' Greta wet, an' Greta wet her pants." Repeated three times.

Later, at fruit, Dorothy said, "I got banana on my nose." Frances: "I got any on the nose. I got any on my nose. I got any on the nose. I got any o'nge juice, I got any o'nge juice." Whether it was the words there or whether she was affected by the facts (for Frances has orange-flavored water and not banana), I do not know.

Looked out of the nursery window and into yards. Began talking: "Oh, see. See all ee peepul, all ee peepul. Oh, see f'owers," etc. Entirely irrelevant; no one in yard, and obviously nothing suggesting flowers is to be seen.

There are various indications that language catches her attention. She tries at new words. An adult was putting her into her sleeping bag and spoke of the ceiling. Frances repeated "skilling" several times. She made various trials, and a day or so later repeated it more nearly like ceiling. Her bag was spread on the dressing table, and then because Patty was ready first, Patty's bag was placed over hers. Frances was disturbed and called, "Das my bag." This was repeated several times, then the adult lifted Patty's and said, "No, Frances, this is yours underneath." Frances was quite satisfied and said, "Mine underneath," over and over. Her habit of repeating phrases used in other connections means something. I believe that the rhythm of phrases catches her.

I have tried to see what other evidences there were of special attention to auditory stimuli, for her language responses probably mean sensitivity to sounds. She turned at the sound of birds chirping, though she could not, or did not, locate them with her eyes. She looks toward and turns toward other children constantly. She was in the nursery and raised her head to look toward the ceiling at the noise of pounding on the roof, noticed roof whistle and chopping in the kitchen. She hears and comments upon music in the gym when she is in the upper hall. Once she noticed crying and recognized Greta's voice proceeding from her bed. The group, sliding, had not attracted her; but she looked up at a squeal from Greta. Planks squeaking caught her attention. She scraped tin pans over tiles, making a peculiarly irritating sound. Harriet and Frances were equally persistent in this pursuit. She drags the coal shovel across the tiles frequently. On the other hand, she does not drop small pans as Sam does, but handles them quietly. When children were allowed to go into room where she was sleeping, she did not wake. Struck Swiss bells in groups of beats in quite regular sequence. (Greta is recorded as striking single bells and waiting until cessation of sound before striking again.) These reactions to the bells have not been repeated.

Frances is also using her language to express to other children her wishes or desires: "No, no, T'a-cy. Can' have it. No, no, T'a-cy, my boo-eel. Frances's boo-eel."

She does little in the way of dramatic play; but as she is covering her doll, she makes remarks about it; there, again, going beyond the actual activities carried on: "See doll crying," and "I put dipees on," were remarks accompanied by no action. She played that her iron was hot. She made passes toward the table and raised a spoon to her mouth as if she were tasting.

Greta's language record is quite different. From the first, her squawking is noted. "Squawks of remonstrance." "A fretting squawk." "A fussing squawk." She does a good deal of this tearless squawking when she wants things, and it is difficult to get past the squawkings to her attention. "No, no, no," in remonstrance. She grunted objection. "A a a a!" was a squawk to get out of the swing. She grunted for help when cart wheels caught, squealed loudly when put on chamber, and squawked in protest when not taken out of bed.

Quite a few words were recorded during the first month (1;8): "Down"; "To'" (toast); "He'ya" (here you are); "Ah we'" (I wet); "Fee" (swing); "Wide" (ride); "Ba-bee" (baby) are examples. "He he," "Ee ee," "A ka da ka ka ka ka," "Ah de be en," "Buh buh buh buh," "Ha uh uh," are examples of her syllabication. There is less range than Frances's, and there seems to be no tendency to arrange syllables into patterns.

On the other hand, she echoes other children's and the adults' intervals: Peter's, Harriet's, Frances's. In February the adult sang the notes, sol sol do. Greta echoed syllables and intervals, but with a quaver in her voice.

Now she has few sentences but is steadily adding to her words. Utility is Greta's impulse.

"Ki ki" (I want to kick.)
"Jump" (I want to jump.)
"Swing" (I want to swing.)
"Ka ka" (I want a cracker.)
"Toas' toas'" (I want toast.)
"Box box" (I want a box.)
"Getty getty" (Get that for me.)
"Han' han'" (hand, hand.)
"My my my my" (That is mine.)
"Me ow a ow" (I want to get out.)
"Catchee catchee" (Catch the ball.)
"How how" (House, house.)
"S'cape" (Scrape.)
"Loo' loo'" (Look.)
"Loo' ow, loo' ow" (Look out.)

She says "No" for the negative and "A-eh" for yes. It is early for the affirmative. She bursts into sentences occasionally. When being unpinned, she said "N-uh one in heah," (Another one in here). She called the adult's attention to a notebook: "Eh's your book. Eh-eh—book—yours—Don." "Cose ee door." If asked a question, she usually repeats a word in it. "Do you want to go to the roof?" "Woof." Her nurse said, "Shall we go in to see the other babies?" Greta: "Ba-bee." Remonstrance, objection, and demand seem to be the usual subjects of Greta's discourses. There is at present little or no play with her words, and no sign that language will run away with her as it does with Frances.

Frances is having more exercise, for her consonant and vowel sounds cover a wider range. I do not believe her pitch and inflection are as varied as Greta's, and I have already noted that her facial muscles are put to less use than Greta's.

Frances sings and murmurs but is less operatic than Greta. As she swung her shoe by the string, she chanted, "Swing, swing." It is entirely impossible to get a record of Greta's quavers and elaborations. Sometimes her voice is cracked and tremulous, and she tends to have a tremolo; but she sings long and varied arias, very tuneful and lovely. She galloped, singing on "luh" in the key of G up to D#; sang for a long time in bed after nap; sings while being dressed; nearly always sings if other children are singing; sings "Down" to accompany her descent of the stairs.

There has been no record for Greta of anything approaching dramatic play.

*Rhythmic activities*

The children give me the impression of being fairly even in their response to music, though it seems to me that Greta has of late made more appropriate responses than Frances. Their records follow, Frances's first:

> *October 6* (1;8) "Brahms Lullaby." Seated on floor with covers. Patted lap in perfect time, then her tempo slowed. Piano was slowed to her pace. She continued for several more beats. Later beat with forefingers, fist closed. Sang a little phrase in the same key, G.
> "Tremp Ton Pain." Stood on chair and trod with alternate feet in practically perfect time, then with right foot alone, then alternate again. Sang also.
> *October 18* (1;9) "En Roulant ma Boule." Very responsive. Sang an octave once. Crept about. Once for many measures walked across room with a long stamping stride (long for her), body and head tipped forward. Very rhythmic and in absolute time.
> She uses her index finger a good deal in response to music. We wonder if her parents have beaten time to music this way. Frances varies her use of fingers in many ways. Once she moved her arms back and forth in time with music, bringing her thrust-out index fingers together in front. Many times she waved her arm with

that finger extended, marking the beat with her whole arm.

*November 9* (1;10)  "Il Etait Une Bergère." Walked in exact time, then made a queer hunching movement with her shoulders rhythmically. Raised shoulders and revolved arms.

*January 3* (1;11)  "Soldier March." Picked up ball and made arm go as though to throw it. Did not, but kept time with the music. Walked with quite a measured tread, lifting one foot high, stepping slightly harder with that foot, and making head go forward and back.

*January 4* (1;11)  To the same selection she made the same sort of response. Crossed arms in front, lifted and lowered them. Seated herself; lifted one foot high; tapped toes on the floor; then swung foot, hitting the floor in time. Did same with the other foot, watching piano.

*January 5* (1;11)  "Birdies." Got down doll covers and, holding one extended, swayed her arms, elbows flexed, and took small steps or tipped up and down on toes. She synchronized arms and legs absolutely, and was in exact time.

In the February and March full-day records she is recorded as making almost no response during the music period. In the weekly summaries the same is true. Mary, the new baby, has required so much attention that the music notes have been scanty; but our impression is that Frances is making fewer responses. She is recorded as "listening" or as giving "attention" to changes or to occasional selections; not invariably to the same ones. "Turkey Buzzard" caught her attention; "Skipping" did also. She did not make rhythmic responses, but either took a listening attitude or changed her activities.

About Greta we have recorded:

*October 21* (1;9) "Minuet." Greta began throwing the ball, then held it extended in hand, fingers up, and kept time for about four beats. Thereafter stood giving a lift to entire trunk and arms as well, exactly with music, though only for a few beats. This was the extent of her response for that period.

Throughout October the records of response from Greta are very scanty.

*November 1* (1;9) "Tremp Ton Pain." Greta did a little gallop step across floor, then exaggerated the dragging of the back foot, stepping with the foot ahead.

Again when the same selection was played, Greta shook a doll's cover up and down for three or four beats.

*November 9* (1;9) "Bergerette." Held a keg hoop in both hands before her and moved it up and down in time with music, often looking toward piano and having a look of interest and attention as if she were beating rhythm occasionally. She has done a similar thing with a cover. Then she started off with her loping step, still holding hoop, one foot ahead of the other, on the beat most of the time.

The next day she walked around and around,

shuffling, dragging a foot, etc. during same selection.

*November 19* (1;10) "Pont d'Avignon." It was played as usual once, then an octave higher and very softly. Greta came with tiny, quick, tip-toe steps across the room, much in the spirit of the music.

"Sun's Bright Red." Waved a cover in perfect time as she sat on the floor.

*December 8* (1;10) "Le Pauvre Enfant." Greta and Harriet kept up a continued trot in varied tempo. Greta had a ball which she turned over and over as she held it with both hands about waist-high. Her "dance figure" was very charming, feet trotting, hands turning ball; but it bore no direct or apparent relationship to the music.

*December 14* (1;11) "Tremp Ton Pain." Greta promptly began to lift shoulders and hands up and down, rising to toes and down again; and then hopped up and down, both feet together and arms waving. Continued, bending knees each time; then played with the ball, tossing it up.

*February 2* (2;0) "Birdies." Greta at once fell into her gallop, in time and in appropriate spirit with the music.

"Soldiers' March." Took a cover by edges and flapped it about in such exact time that it seemed impossible for her to have done it.

There were numerous other records of brief responses from Frances and Greta. They both show sensitivity to sound, and until Frances's lapse during February and March, after her long illness in January, their responses were fairly similar, controlled and governed by the differences in their musculature.

*Social activities*

The social reactions of the two children are very different. Frances has a certain dependence on adults which is shown in her habit of asking for materials or for help when she needs none. She will take an adult's hand, lead her to the slide, and then wait. A few days ago she asked for covers which were on a closet shelf. When a chair was placed to aid her in reaching them, she stood before it, putting up one foot tentatively, behaving as if she were entirely unequal to stepping on to it. She was helped, but immediately after, climbed up and down, with very good technique and comparatively little hesitation.

Her recent drive on C B is an exaggerated instance of her efforts to concentrate adult attention upon herself. In this case she seems to want an affectionate or a play response, not definite help. She shows this attitude only toward C B but does not resist attention from others of the nursery staff. A more or less determined drive to get her attention was started seven times during her most recent full-day record. Attention was also given the recorder, but of quite another variety.

She carries on little babyish games with separate individuals. On occasion she has joined in the ball throwing, but still has such an inadequate technique that she cannot join on equal terms with the others. She enjoys watching group play but is not likely to

get involved in it. She has a peculiar method of joining activities on the side lines. In November (1;10)
the following incident was noted:

> Several children were bouncing on the planks
> laid from sandbox to tiles. Frances, on a flat one,
> followed actions of others. Moved and bobbed
> or turned on her stationary board, quite a mem-
> ber of the group, though entirely outside of it.

In her last full-day record there is a similar account.
She seems more at ease in this type of group activity
than when she is in a position in which she is compet-
ing with the other children, especially in maintaining
balance.

Frances can carry on play, like peek-a-boo or
chasing, with a single other child; but numbers seem
to disturb her. Greta plunges into group situations,
especially ones of full-bodied vigorous play. Frances
watches a great deal and, as remarked, simulates
group play by herself. There are about as many ref-
erences in recent records to her watching as to
Greta's, but her subsequent action is different.

> *February 2* (2;0) Frances watches a good deal
> but is not often moved by what she sees of
> children's activity to join them. For instance, for
> four successive days Tracy and Sam joined
> Harriet at her table over toast and water—their
> nuts and wine. Frances showed no impulse to
> do so. (Greta absent.)

In a summary report the following note appears:

> Greta's social advances were commented on

at the staff meeting at which she was discussed. She seems to get her impulse to activity from things she sees other children doing. However, it is not the purely social, that is, the contacts with other children, which seems to interest Greta as much as the activities which they are carrying on. It seems to us that Greta is gaining abilities and control of her body by this method; and as time goes on, she is showing much less susceptibility to distraction. She is able to become absorbed in an activity of her own and shows quite a long span of interest.

Patty's jumping, Peter's jumping, Sam's interlocking blocks, and the methods used by the older children in sliding, have been subjects for Greta's experimentation. She slides both head-first and sitting, on the indoor slide as well as the outdoor; and she walked up and down the slide chute when it was elevated on the sawhorse. She has learned through a progressively maturing pattern to interlock blocks. Both she and Frances have attempted using the shelves as sleeping berths, in imitation of the older children. She has at last been able to get into the lower berth and lie down. Very persistent in her efforts to get off her feet in jumping, she has taken a few leaps that cleared the floor. She plays a very good ball game, throwing overhand with fair aim and holding her interest over a decent period. Frances does not yet throw but drops the ball into the hands of her partner. This seems to indicate that in the case of Greta the impulse to "imitate" older children has been arising from a sufficiently integrated neuro-muscular equipment so that a learning process has been set up by means of it. If we compare Elizabeth's behavior at eighteen, twenty-two, and twenty-three months, we shall see that the same apparent impulse was a very disintegrating influence on her activity. She was too immature to be aware of the processes carried on by the older children and saw only the materials in their hands.

Greta shows none of the dependence upon adults that is characteristic of Frances. She is friendly and responsive, but controlled. She does not initiate affectionate demonstration but, if an adult makes advances to her, responds, if her attention is sufficiently disengaged at the time. The sort of bid she makes for adult attention is shown when she is alone with them. Then she will take poses or do her gallop or her jumping about, pausing to watch adults between her efforts. She laughs loudly if they respond. There is little opportunity for this sort of play in the nursery, and Greta never lets it interrupt her drive toward materials and children.

*Immaturities*

There are certain immaturities shown by each of the children.

Greta's language and her ability to respond to language stimuli are much less developed than Frances's. We have repeated records of Frances's responding on the instant not only to a direction like "Turn around," but also to a direction implied in the remark of one adult to another.

Greta's lack of bladder control is in sharp contrast to Frances's, who can be trusted when she refuses toilet at usual intervals. Greta's intervals are short and not regularly established.

Frances has not, up to date, been able to place her chair successfully at her table. She has repeatedly placed it with the back toward the table and has given up the problem. She cannot deal with the situation of a chair placed too far away from the table, but reaches over as best she may.

> *March 1* (2;1) Frances was asked to put her chair at the table. She pulled it an inch or so toward table and seated herself. She was not satisfied. It was off at the side and a foot away. She stood and lifted chair, her hands under seat as she sat on it. Did not straighten up but kept buttocks in the seat. With great effort, drew a few inches nearer table. Encouraged by adult, she rose and pushed chair up, this time into better position. Said, "Fis' it dis way." Seated herself and made no effort to pull the table up nearer.

This is much the best performance she has given.

In the record of December 21 (1;11), Greta is recorded as placing her chair under the table, then pulling it out sideways so that she could sit on it. Also has placed two yard-blocks accurately enough to make a seat.

————

This lengthy report has attempted to give outstanding differences in the two children as we see them reacting to situations in the nursery school environment.

What does the difference in physical development mean? For once dentition and carpal development seem to run together. Frances is ahead of her age in the latter at least; Greta is behind in dentition, and the process seems to affect her digestion and the whole naso-pharyngeal tract. Frances is believed to have an infected area in her nose and throat, and that may explain her reluctances toward certain types of active play.

Is it possible that she has a vision defect? She showed marked vertigo after swinging in the knotted rope early in the year, but has persisted in her experimentation with it and shows no such tendency now. Greta has never shown dizziness.

What is the next step toward an understanding of relationships?*

* Space does not permit the inclusion of staff discussion which followed immediately upon presentation of reports such as these.

The above studies illustrate one use to which detailed records of children's behavior can be put. What Harriet Johnson hoped to attain through painstaking recording can be stated in her own words:

> We are attempting to study the reactions of children to their environment, what they do to the environment, how they adapt the materials and persons in it to their own purposes, and what the environment does to them, how their behavior is modified by conditions which they find or which their own reactions bring about. These are fundamental problems in education and in psychology, and we are still in the initial stages of attack upon them. In the nature of the case a discussion of our records is not in terms of reaction time to definite stimuli; it does not involve the method of presenting a controlled laboratory situation with its result. We are attempting to study a child's individual and characteristic way of responding to situations set up by the nursery school environment. We are calling his way of reacting his behavior pattern in regard to this or that situation. We realize that there may be no observable beginning and end to a given response, that there is implicit as well as overt behavior, of which we may remain entirely unaware, or the implications of which we may trace in posture, in random movements or in a speeding up of the learning process. We record what we can observe and we isolate for our purposes the portion of the child's response

which seems to have to do with the situation under observation. Such a procedure is demanded by the limits of human powers of analysis. If we did not define our problem we should have only a mass of unrelated observations.

Children come into the nursery school with very immature perceptual development in regard to many of the objects and situations which they find there. Before they leave they have set up many different habitual modes of response, indicating progress in the awareness of meanings in their dealing with such objects and situations. We are trying to record the development of their patterned responses—the earliest tentative attempt to set up a pattern, the degree of persistence after it is initiated and the way it is elaborated and matured.

Following are the sources from which excerpts have been taken and assembled for the several sections of this book. *The Working Background of Harriet Johnson's Contribution to Education* has been adapted from an article by Lucy Sprague Mitchell entitled "Harriet Johnson, Pioneer," published in Progressive Education, November, 1934. Harriet Johnson was the author of all the papers, published and unpublished, which are listed below. The section on *Foundations for a School Philosophy* has drawn upon the following:

Educational Implications of the Nursery School, Progressive Education, Jan.-Feb.-Mar., 1925.

The Education of the Nursery School Child, Childhood Education, November, 1926.

Responsibilities for the Young Child, Child Study, January, 1928.

Talks to Parents' Council of Philadelphia, 1929.

Paper for Symposium on Thumb-Sucking, Child Study, April, 1930.

Courtesy and Manners, Talk to Parent Group, Windward School, 1930.

Sources for the material assembled in the section on *Working Hypotheses of a Nursery School* follow:

Mental Hygiene of Younger Children. Paper presented at National Conference of Social Work, Toronto, 1924.

Paper contributed to 28th Yearbook, National Society for the Study of Education, 1929.

Talks to Parents' Council of Philadelphia, 1929.

Emotional Life of Children in Nursery School, Notes for talk to Child Study Group, 1930.

Pioneer Babies in the New Education, American Childhood, February, 1930.

Play Materials for the Preschool Child, American Childhood, December, 1930.

Creative Materials for the Preschool Child, American Childhood, January, 1931.

Dramatic Play in the Nursery School, Progressive Education, January, 1931.

Talk to American Association of University Women, April, 1931.

Progressive Teachers, Radio Address, 1932.

The quotation at the close of the book is taken from "Children in the Nursery School" by Harriet M. Johnson, published in 1928 by The John Day Company, New York.

We wish to make acknowledgment to Louise P. Woodcock who, for eight years, was an active member of Miss Johnson's staff, for her valuable cooperation in organizing Part III and in preparing the manuscript for print.